Abused

Assume Nothing

**Eight stories
of children murdered by
their parents or caregivers**

Jessica Jackson

This work is based on real cases

*The first part of each story is semi-fictionalised,
with some events and dialogue added*

*The second part tells the facts of each case,
detailing the injuries, trials and sentencing*

Copyright Jessica Jackson © 2021 All rights reserved
No part of this book may be reproduced in any form
without written permission from the author
Reviewers may quote brief passages in reviews

*For the purposes of anonymity, names of
siblings and friends have been changed
unless where commonly known*

This book has details of child abuse
that some readers may find upsetting

Printed by Amazon
In the unlikely event of errors being made during
the printing process, they will be happy to replace your book

Simply go to Your Orders, Replace
and be sure to write 'faulty' across the cover
before returning your book

*Cover photograph of Baby P
by kind permission
of the copyright holder*

Contents

Hi From Jessica 5

Your Free E-Book... 6

Mummy, Daddy. Please stop! 7

Blue Eyes... 9

Who Tortures Children? 50

Get Me Out of Here... 53

The Abuser's Childhood.. 75

A Family Christmas... 77

A Child is a Human Being! 106

The Punch-Bag 109

Returning Children to their Abuser 134

The Bit in the Middle 136

Warning Signs of Abuse 137

Homeschool... 139

The Homeschool Debate 165

Fit For A Mother's Love.. 167

Who's To Blame? 196

Blowtorch 199

When Did Child Abuse Begin? 219

A Mouthful of Swede 221

Physical Discipline 234

Help To Protect Children …... 238

Your Next Book in the Series.. 239

Join Us On Facebook 240

Hello (again!) from Jess 241
Readers' List Benefits..242
Pick Up Your Free E-Book and Join Us!........................243
Find All My Books on Amazon......................................244
Don't Miss A Thing 245
Easy Review Codes 246
Acknowledgments 247
Selected Resources 248

Hi From Jessica

Hi, I'm Jess – thank you for choosing my first book.

Although I've always loved reading and writing, I never imagined I'd write my own books. But when I realised that thousands of children are dying every year at the hands of their caregivers, I felt I *had* to write their stories, with a view to awareness and prevention.

> If you can spare a moment when you've finished reading, I'd be very grateful if you'd help to raise awareness of child abuse by rating or reviewing this book.

I also have a FREE ebook for you.

You can check it out overleaf …

JESSICA JACKSON

Your Free E-Book

Exclusive only to my readers

**The tragic case
of Isaiah Torres**

*(with bonus content about
Baby Brianna Lopez)*

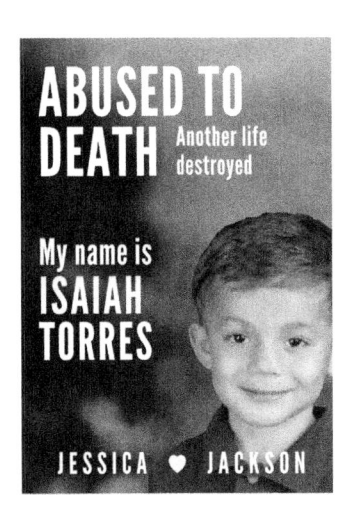

ABUSED TO DEATH Another life destroyed

My name is ISAIAH TORRES

JESSICA ♥ JACKSON

I'll let you know how to get your copy later

*(Royalties from my books go to
NSPCC, UNICEF and
Prevent Child Abuse America)*

Mummy, Daddy. Please stop!

A CHILD'S PLEA. One that we don't want to believe is real. A parent harming their own child, to the point of torture and murder? Surely this can't be happening?

But thousands of children have no escape from their parents or caregivers, and are abused to death.

We hear about the high profile cases and we assume this crime is extremely rare. But we are wrong; 2 children die from abuse and neglect almost every week in the UK, and in the US, the figure is a staggering 27 per week.

But my book is about children, not statistics, and I tell most of the stories in two parts; the first being a semi-fictionalised story based firmly on the facts, and the second detailing the injuries, the trial and sentencing.

By giving a voice to those who were silenced, Abused To Death honours the memory of the children, and looks for ways we can prevent these dreadful crimes.

- A – Assume nothing
- B – Be vigilant
- C – Check everything
- D – Do something

And LISTEN to the children

JESSICA JACKSON

Blue Eyes

'You okay, babes?' My father scrapes back her damp, dark brown hair, then grasps her hand.

'I'm absolutely shattered,' says my mother, flopping back onto the sweat-soaked pillows. 'But we've got a boy. At last.'

'I know, it's fantastic,' says Daddy. 'Well done, love.'

The midwife starts to hand me to my mother, but she folds her arms, scowling slightly.

Daddy steps in quickly. 'Let me hold him. Oh, he's gorgeous! Isn't he, Tracey?'

'Yeah. Yes, he is. I'm so tired though.' She turns onto her side; her back to Daddy and me.

'Oh God, 'course you are. You have a good rest. Do you want to give him a quick cuddle before you go to sleep?'

'No, it's okay. There's plenty of time for that.'

'You need to bond with him, Trace. Remember how it was with the girls.'

'I know, I know.'

Daddy cradles me gently, his warm breath on my ear. 'It'll be okay this time, son.'

Once we're back home, whenever Daddy's around, she strokes my cheek and calls me her beautiful blue-eyed boy, and Daddy looks at us both with a huge grin.

'A boy, Tracey.' It's like Daddy can't believe his luck. He holds out his arms to gather in my three sisters. 'And our gorgeous girls.' Reminding them to be careful, he lets my sisters snuggle and kiss me.

'Will he grow as big as you, Daddy?'

'Oh, yes! Maybe even bigger!'

My oldest sister puts her hands on her hips and cocks her head to the side, frowning a little. 'Really, Daddy?'

He reaches out and tickles her. 'Yes, really, Miss Cheeky-Face.'

'I love him already,' she says.

Mummy's face has turned dark. 'What do you mean? How can you love him when all he does is shit and drink milk?'

'I know, but ...' She seems to know better than to say any more.

'And don't be cuddling him all the time. You're going to make him soft.'

'Don't say that, Tracey,' says Daddy. 'Remember what the midwife said. Look, he's already trying to smile when I pick him up and rock him. Here, you give it a try.'

But my mother swings me too fast and Daddy has to grab me away from her.

'Go gently, Trace. You were practically shaking him.'

'Well, you try looking after four of them, then!'

'I'm not getting at you, babes. I know it can't be easy. But I want you all to be okay when I'm back at work next week.'

'Oh, don't worry; we'll be fine!'

'Yeah, you will,' he says. 'Hey, you look tired again, babes.'

'I am a bit.' She sighs. 'Will you go and get me some fags?'

As soon as Daddy goes out, she starts pinching and poking me. And when I cry she yells at me to shut up, and slaps my face. She strokes my head when she hears the key in the door.

'Bloody hell, Trace, I could hear him all the way down the street! What's the matter with him?'

'He's always like this when you're not here.' As she hands me to Daddy, she glowers at the girls, with a warning to keep their mouths shut.

'Ahh, son. What's the matter, hey? Shush now, Daddy's here.'

I do shush. And I'm so glad Daddy's here.

'Get out! Just get the hell out!' My mother has been yelling at Daddy for a long time.

My sisters are standing in the corner, not daring to move.

'I don't want you here!'

'Quieten down, Tracey. We can sort things out calmly.'

'I don't want to be quiet.'

'If you'd just listen. We both want the same thing. I don't like this any more than you do.'

'Don't you?'

'No, I don't. We both know this isn't working anymore.'

'Oh?' She drops the knife and her glare softens.

'Come on, sit down. Let's talk.'

It's peaceful in the house for the first time in ages.

Daddy is holding Mummy's hand. 'I'll always be there for the kids, Trace. You won't shut me out, will you?'

She shrugs. 'Yeah, whatever.'

'I mean it, Tracey. I love those kids. You know that.'

'I suppose so.'

'I'll still be a good help to you. And I don't just mean with money. I'll take the kids out; give you a break.'

She lights up another cigarette, and reaches for a bottle. 'Want a quick swig?'

'No, no I don't, love. And you shouldn't ...'

'Are you getting on at me again?'

'It's just when you're taking care of the kids. Maybe when they've gone to bed?'

'You don't run my life! This is why I want you out of here!'

'Shh, Tracey. Please, just be sensible.'

She pours herself a large one and slumps back in her chair.

'I'll put the kids to bed then,' says Daddy. 'Come on, little fella. And you girls. Say "night-night" to Mummy.'

She wafts her hand at us. 'Sod off to bed.'

'Hi, Tracey.'

'Hi, Angela. Come in, if you can get past all this mess.'

'How're you coping on your own?'

'It's bloody hard work.' She turns to my middle sister. 'Hey, get down off that chair.'

Her friend nods. 'Little buggers, aren't they?'

'They've got that many bumps and bruises I bet they'll end up taking them off me.'

'Don't be daft, Tracey. Some kids play rough, and some bruise really easy.' She tickles my tummy. 'The social workers know that. Don't worry. You're a good mum, Trace.'

'But even the little un's got marks on him.'

'Well, you'll have to watch his big sisters. Maybe they think he's their new toy!'

My mother shrugs.

'Come on, Tracey. Give us a smile. Hey, you've got to admit, he is like a little doll. And those blue eyes. You'd better watch out; he's going to be a real heartbreaker.'

'Jesus, Angela! He's just a baby, not a bloody miracle.'

Angela's not listening. She lifts my hand and kisses it. 'Aww, look at his tiny finger nails.'

Mummy is muttering to herself as she shuts the door on her friend. 'Does she *have* to be so damn cheerful all the time? I'd like to see her deal with four whining kids and housework and bills and stuff.' She leans back in her chair and looks across at us. 'Where's that remote control? Who the hell's hidden it?'

My three sisters stand in the middle of the room, rooted to the spot.

'Where the hell is it?' she asks my biggest sister. 'Oh, Jesus Christ, you lot are gonna drive me up the wall. If you don't find that remote by the time I've counted to ten, you know what you're in for.'

My littlest sister is trying to hide her sobs behind her sleeve, but Mummy whirls on her.

'I'll give you something to cry about, lady, if you don't shut up. Right, just get out, all of you. Get to bed.'

The little girls run, toddle and crawl out of the room, and our mother looks down at me, clenching her fists.

After she's had a little drink of vodka she takes me out of the pram and puts me on her knee, drumming her fingers up and down my arms and legs. Then she gropes down the side of the cushion, and holds up the remote in triumph. She clicks the button and scans the channels, and starts up with the prodding and pinching again, slapping me if I so much as whimper.

The day after next she's on the phone to her friend; more upbeat than she's been in a while. 'Hey, Ange. I've met someone.'

Daddy and me are out in the park with his best friend.

'Yeah, 'course I'm happy for her, Wayne. But I haven't met him, so I don't know what he's like around the kids.'

'Hey, come on. He'll be great with them. If it's the same Barker who went to my school, he was just a big soft lump.'

'What, like a gentle giant, sort of thing?'

'Well, I wouldn't go that far. I remember his older brother used to boss him around a fair bit.'

'Poor kid; now he'll have Tracey doing the same!'

Wayne laughs. 'You're well out of that one, mate.'

'Ahh, she's just young, that's all. Mind you, she has got a short fuse at times.' Daddy lifts me out of the pram for a cuddle. 'I've heard this Barker fella's never seen without his Rottweiler?'

'Trying to make himself look hard, that's all.'

'Big dog to have around the little uns though.'

'I suppose so. But do the kids seem happy enough?'

'Yeah. Yeah, they seem fine. And it's not like he's going to be living there or anything.'

'There you go then. Just keep an eye on things.'

'I will. But she's already starting to shut me out. So I daren't say too much, or she might stop me seeing the kids.' He blows a raspberry on my cheek.

'Even Tracey wouldn't do that,' says Wayne. 'Now stop your worrying.'

Everything changes in November when Steven comes to live with us.

Mummy belts us kids, of course. But we know it's coming because her face starts to go dark and she shouts really loud; usually because one of us doesn't move quick enough when she says, 'Get to bed, you little runts.'

But with Steven, there doesn't have to be a reason. He pounds my head, and calmly waits for my reaction; it's usually screaming. He makes my sister take her clothes off and she says, 'Mummy, please make him stop.' But Mummy doesn't help her. She just sits watching the computer or the TV. And there's men and ladies on the TV doing things like Steven does to my sister. My sister's screams make the dog bark and the neighbours bang on the walls. But he still doesn't stop. Not for a long time. When he finally does he throws her into the corner, and me into my cot, where I bang my head against the bars so that I don't notice how hungry I am. Sometimes he towers above me, just watching.

'Little toe-rag,' he says, grabbing me by the back of the head and ramming a dummy into my mouth so hard it makes my lips bleed.

By December, I have to go into hospital because of all the bruises. Mostly on my face, but on my neck and chest too. Ooh, the nurses are lovely! They smell so clean and touch me so gently. Mummy gets really mad though, because a policeman arrests her, and I'm not allowed to go back home. I have to go and stay with Angela. Angela's not as rough as Mummy, and of course there's no Steven, so it's pretty great for a few weeks.

One day a curly-haired lady comes in a big, new car, and Angela cuddles me while the lady asks her a lot of questions. 'How old is he now, Angela?'

'Nine months.'

'Hmm, he's a bit underweight for his age, but his bruises have all faded now,' says the lady. 'And there doesn't seem to be any new ones.'

'Yeah, Tracey says he's very clumsy if you take your eye off him for a second. But I've been able to watch him more closely, so he doesn't keep having these accidents.'

'Hmm, about these accidents. What do you think's been causing them?'

'Well, like I say, he's clumsy, and Tracey says his sisters play a bit rough with him.'

'I see.' The lady is writing everything down. 'But what do *you* think, Angela?'

Angela shrugs. 'It's obvious, isn't it? His sisters aren't here, so he doesn't get bruised as much.'

A few days later, the curly-haired lady comes back and straps me into the baby-seat in her car.

Mummy has put away the vodka bottles and cleaned up the kitchen, but I can still smell where the dog does its business on the living room carpet. She even cuddles me, and there's no sign of Steven. My two oldest sisters have learnt some songs at school, so they rock me and sing 'Baa baa black sheep' and 'Twinkle, twinkle, little star'. We all eat some kind of toffee pudding, and when I get myself all sticky, Mummy just wipes it off. She doesn't even shout.

But the next night, he's back. He says that all the trouble with the police and children's services was my fault, and I need to be punished. My head whips back when he throws the first punch, but I soon black out.

He's got a new party trick. 'Hey, Tracey. Watch this.' He clicks his fingers and I cringe and lower my head right down to the floor. His dog is doing the same.

She's killing herself laughing. 'You're a nutter, Steven! What're you doing to the little devil?'

He kicks me in the back. 'Just showing him who's boss, Tracey. Just showing him who's boss.' When he throws me into my cot later on, I lie there for a while before I start banging my head against the bars. It hurts; quite a bit. But it soothes the other places where I hurt more.

I wish Steven would go away again. Far away, and never come back.

They've organised some help for my mother. Well, quite a lot of help; I'm going to a child-minder four days a week. And it's brilliant! Ann looks after my sister and a couple of other kids too, and I learn how to play and to say some words. I love Ann's house. It's so clean and it smells nice. The other day when we were in the kitchen, and I was reaching up for a biscuit, she told me to hang on while she took my photograph.

'Let's get a picture of those big blue eyes,' she said.

'They match his jumper,' said my sister.

'You're right, sweetheart,' said Ann. 'And doesn't he look gorgeous against my black and white tiled floor?'

I tried to say the word 'gorgeous', and we all started giggling.

I love going to the park and playing on the swings. It's lovely to be outside. With my sister on the swing next to me, and Ann pushing each of us in turn, I get a warm feeling inside and a smile on my face.

'You happy, Peter?' says Ann.

Going on the school run with Ann is great too. I feel nice and secure when I'm strapped in the car, with Ann singing nursery rhymes and us kids joining in.

Sometimes though, I just want to stand in Ann's hallway on my own. I feel safe near the front door, and wonder if I could run away if Steven came to get me.

Ann doesn't make me go back into her living room to play with the other kids. 'Hey, little man,' she says, handing me a biscuit. 'I wonder what it's like for you at home.'

It's awful there, Ann. Please can you keep me here with you all the time?

'Another bruise on your cheek.' She sighs. 'But you don't seem to fall and bump into things much when you're here.'

And I don't do it at home either, Ann. Please, please tell somebody.

'And this banging your head on the wall and the floor. It's just not right. I definitely need to let children's services know.' She goes away for a minute and comes back with the big teddy and holds him up to her ear.

'What's that, Teddy? You want Peter to give you a big cuddle?'

I hold out my arms.

'Teddy wants to stay here with you for a while. Is that okay?'

I nod and bury my face in his soft, white fur.

Ann puts her arms round both of us and kisses the top of my head. 'Poor little mite,' she says.

Ann is on the doorstep, talking to the two other mummies.

'It's just not healthy, Ann,' one of them is saying. 'I'll have to find someone else if you can't sort it.'

The other lady is nodding.

'I know, I know,' says Ann. 'It's not their fault though. And I can keep an eye on things, you know, while they're coming here.'

The other mummies glance at me. 'I'm sorry, Ann. I feel terrible about this, but you know how quickly lice get passed from one head to another, and before we know it, it'll be all over my older one's school. I just can't take that chance, Ann.'

'Listen, I'll get them to cut their hair, even shave it right down. I'm sure I'll be able to get rid of the little buggers.'

The two mummies shrug. 'We'll see. But it's just not right, Ann.'

A week later, Ann and my sister are crying. 'I'm sorry, sweetheart. I'd keep you both if I could. But we just can't get rid of those naughty things. Do you think Peter understands?'

I'm hiding my face behind the big teddy.

'Come here, love. Give your Auntie Ann a big hug. Let your sister take Teddy.'

She holds me close for a while, and I can feel her shaking. Then she blows her nose and reaches for my coat. 'Your mummy will be here soon.'

We don't get ready to go to Ann's the next day. Or any other day after that.

Now I know that other kids aren't kicked and punched and yelled at all day long, I keep hoping that my mother and Steven will change. But things get worse, if anything. Finally, the social worker notices the swelling on my head and the scratches all over my face and body. My mother is arrested again, and I go to hospital. It's almost as good as being at Ann's house.

I sleep in a cot with white sheets and am allowed to eat and drink whenever I want.

'Where's my little sweetheart?'

Which one of the nurses is that? I think I'm going to get a cuddle. It hurts a lot every time I'm moved but I don't care.

'Ooh, I could keep you here for ever.'

Will you? Please?

But the kindness and warmth are soon over, and I'm back in the hands of my mother and Steven.

Steven has an older brother. I hoped he'd be gentle and kind like my older sisters, and stop Steven doing horrible things to us. But he doesn't.

I remember the day he moved in, with his girlfriend, some more kids, and his pets.

My mother is busy watching the TV, and stuffing her face with crisps and vodka.

Steven's saying, 'No, I mean it, bro. Absolutely anything. She doesn't give a damn.'

Jason licks his lips. 'Well okay then! Let's have a good look at the little runt.'

He dangles me by my hair and nappy above the dogs and snakes, then swoops me down towards them.

My screaming makes my mother turn round for a second. 'Nutters!' She goes back to the screen.

Jason throws me onto the coffee table. 'Stop staring at me, you little monster.'

I close my eyes, and he punches my head.

'Did I say you could shut your soddin' eyes? Did I?'

When I open them, he's an inch from my face. 'Now keep them open.'

'I thought you didn't like him looking at you, bro,' says Steven. 'You said you hated his bright blue eyes.'

'Oh, I do. I hate everything about the little brat. But what I like, what I really, really like ...' He grabs my chin and squeezes. 'Is seeing how bloody terrified he looks now I've got my hands on him.'

'Yeah, it's good, isn't it?' says Steven.

'Right, let's have a proper look. Now what have we here? Don't you ever cut his finger nails?'

Steven flushes. 'Well, we just ...'

'No worries, bro. I'm not complaining. You ever tried pliers on him?'

Steven shakes his head.

'Well go and get some, you dork. A small pair.'

They clamp the pliers onto my finger nails and twist. When they get tired of my screaming they shove an old sock in my mouth. They take it out when I pass out. They don't want to kill me. Where's the fun in that?

My mother wraps my hands in bandages when I go out for the day with my daddy.

Daddy, take the bandages off. Please Daddy, look what they're doing to me. I've got no finger nails.

But I'm not good at talking yet and I can't tell him. When we're in the café I plunge my hands into the chocolate ice-cream to dirty the bandages. *Come on, Daddy. Look at the mess I've made. Why don't you shout at me and take the bandages off?*

'Oh son, that's naughty,' he smiles. And he just shakes his head, wipes the bandages with a serviette and spoons me another mouthful.

After the café we go to the swings I used to go to with Ann, but I don't feel like playing.

'Hey, what's up, son?' He wraps his arms round me and hugs me. 'You don't want to go on the swings?' He sits down on the bench and bounces me gently on his knee. 'We can just sit here and watch the other kids then, can't we son?'

It feels so good to be in Daddy's arms, so I don't know why I'm crying. I snuggle into him and hide my face in his chest.

'Aww, you love your Daddy, don't you?'

'Yes,' I say quietly, into the folds of his jumper.

Daddy's handing me back to her and I'm screaming. 'Daddy, Daddy, Daddy.' I can't go back in there, I just can't. I hold out my arms to him and he hunches up his shoulders. 'Sorry, son. That's all I get with you. I'll see you next week.' He turns to her. 'Hey Tracey, is he okay?'

'He's fine.'

I twist my head right round and he's still standing at the gate, like he doesn't want to leave me, and he's doing one of those funny little waves, with just his fingers.

Bye, Daddy.

The door slams.

'I think he's been trying to say stuff.'

'Stuff?'

'Y'know.' She turns back to watching naked men and ladies on the computer.

Steven grabs me and I whirl through the air and smash against the wall. I know my screaming eggs them on, but I can't stop.

'I'm sick of that racket,' says Jason. 'Set the dog on him. Hey, Kaiser, get here.'

Tracey looks round from her computer with that vacant expression. 'Hey, what you doing with him?'

'Shut up, bitch. He needs toughening up.'

She turns away. Again.

Steven and Jason are out at the pub, and my mother's got a friend here. She's told me not to cry or bang my head in front of the friend, but she hasn't ruled out sitting near her and feeling her warmth.

'I know I shouldn't laugh,' my mother is saying. 'But sometimes when Steven's messing with him, he looks so scared, and it's a bit like he's trying to escape.'

'Poor little sod.'

Not great, but I've been called worse.

'I know. But he can't get away. He's hardly been three feet away from Steven since the day he moved in.'

'Bit of a head-case, isn't he, your fella?'

'Oh God, yeah. And his brother's just the same. Worse, maybe. To be honest, when they start with the kids I sometimes have to look away.'

'But you don't let them hurt them, Tracey? Not really?'

She doesn't miss a beat. 'Oh no, 'course not. What do you think I am!'

The next time the social worker comes they've smeared chocolate and cream all over my face to hide the cuts and bruises. Underneath the cute little hat, my ear is practically torn off, where the brothers had some fun with my head and a pair of pliers.

The social worker doesn't notice that my some of my ribs are broken. And that Steven had laid me across his knee while he was watching the telly and casually snapped my back. I think she just thinks I'm being grumpy when I cry out in pain. Still, I have an appointment tomorrow with a doctor at a place called the Child Development Clinic. Been waiting months for it. They're specially trained to look out for kids like me, so at last, I'm pretty sure I'm gonna be rescued.

The waiting room is bursting with crying toddlers. When it's finally our turn, the doctor calls the receptionist in to ask where my notes are. The young girl shrugs.

'Okay, let's see what we can manage today without them,' says the doctor. 'And then we'll have you back in when I've got the background information I need.' She touches my cheek gently. 'I don't like the look of these bruises on his face, Mrs Connelly.'

'He's a clumsy little devil,' says my mother. 'Falls into the furniture all the time.'

'Yes, I suppose he's at that age when they start toddling everywhere, and getting into mischief.' She shuffles the papers on her desk. 'How old is Peter, Mrs Connelly?'

'Seventeen months.'

The doctor smiles at me, but when she tries to move my legs I scream. 'I'm sorry, Peter,' she says. 'But I need to examine you.'

'He's just not well today,' says my mother helpfully.

'I'll try again.' The doctor lifts my leg, but it's unbearable.

'You're right,' she says. 'And I don't have any information on him at all. What can you tell me about his injuries?'

My mother shrugs.

The doctor tries with me. 'Where does it hurt, Peter?'

I wish I could tell her. I hurt everywhere. But I don't know how to explain, and my mother is glaring at me. And Steven's just outside, in the waiting room.

'Okay, then. I'll gather what information I can, and then see him again in a few days.'

My mother grabs me (more screaming) and we're out of the door in a flash.

Steven stands up as we head back into the waiting room. 'What a fuckin' racket,' he says, throwing me into my pushchair. 'I can't wait to sort him out when we get him home.' As we get outside, he punches my face to remind me what to expect.

'Steven!' says my mother. 'The doctor's already mentioned his bruises. And we have to bring him back here in a few days.'

'They're our bloody kids, Tracey. It's up to us how we deal with them, not some useless doctor.'

'I don't want them to take him off me again, though. It's such a pain, and my ex will be nosying around as usual, asking questions.'

'Alright, alright. Me and Jason'll find a way to give him hell without marking him much.'

'Yeah, okay. Don't hurt him too much though, babes. If we're not careful, he's going to manage to tell somebody.'

He looks down at me. 'You won't tell, will you, Peter? Because you know you'll only get it a lot worse if you do.'

That evening, Steven and Jason show me what they mean by 'a lot worse'. When I call out for my daddy, Jason bangs his fist onto my fingers and yells at me to 'shut the fuck up'. I scream for Ann too, and the nurses and doctors who looked after me. I don't call for my mother.

When she finds me in my cot the next day I'm already blue and stiff. She's too spaced out to panic and the brothers seem quite proud of themselves. They think they can get away with murder.

I wish I'd had the chance to grow up. To get as tall as Daddy said I would, so that I could protect my sisters against people like Barker and his brother. And I'd ask our mother why she hurt us so much, and why she stood by as it grew into torture.

The whole country was shocked at what they did to me. I hope they'll remember, and look out for other kids like me. In my memory, hundreds of people let off blue balloons which flew high into the sky. And even before they knew my name, and I was still known as Baby P, someone paid for my simple black headstone. It says all it needs to say on there: *Safe at last*.

An Overview of Peter's Case

Peter Connelly (Baby P)

01.03.06 - 03.08.07

aged 1 year and 5 months

London, England

The little boy, initially known to the public as Baby P, was tortured to death at the age of 17 months, by his mother Tracey Connelly, her boyfriend Steven Barker, and Barker's brother Jason Owen. Peter had more than fifty injuries at the time of his death, many of which are said to defy human understanding. Peter's story is possibly the best known case of torture and murder of a child by his/her caregivers in the UK.

§

Peter was the fourth child, and only son, of Tracey Connelly and her husband. (The name of Peter's birth father has not been revealed.) The couple split up approximately three months after Peter was born, although they later reconciled, before separating for good. It is my understanding that Mr Connelly was a responsible father who continued to pay support for his children after the split. After a short while, Tracey's new boyfriend, Steven Barker, moved into the family home. The pair successfully hid the fact that they were cohabiting from the authorities, so that Tracey would continue to receive welfare benefits.

§

Tracey Connelly's own childhood was far from idyllic. Raised in Islington by a neglectful mother, neighbours claimed that Tracey and her older brother were unkempt and uncared for, and that the filthy house had dog faeces on the floor. Journalist Andrew Anthony, who wrote for The Observer and The Guardian newspapers, interviewed Tracey's mother, Mary O'Connor, in 2009, and reveals that child neglect stems from even further back. O'Connor was only four days old when her mother died, and five years old when her stepmother died, and she was so frightened of her father that she used to wet herself in his presence. Beaten by him, and sexually abused by a relative when she was nine, she ran away from home at the age of thirteen. O'Connor's father had been raised in an orphanage, and his own childhood is likely to have been instrumental in schooling him in the brutality he dished out to his offspring.

Mr Anthony's report, entitled 'Baby P: born into a nightmare of abuse, violence and despair, he never stood a chance', details a catalogue of neglect and violence echoing down the decades, which he says serves as 'a graphic warning of the horrors that generations of neglect and savage abuse can visit on children'.

Tracey herself was placed on the child protection register, and spent her teenage years at a boarding school for troubled children, before meeting her husband, a man in his thirties, at the age of sixteen.

Following the births of their four children, Tracey and her husband separated, although their father tried to remain a supportive presence in his children's lives.

§

Steven Barker, the second eldest of five siblings, grew up torturing animals for kicks, which led to him being prosecuted by the RSPCA. He grew to six feet four inches tall, but the blond haired youth had an IQ of only 60. He became fanatical about Nazism, and owned a cross-bow and various martial arts weapons.

Barker is said to have been dominated by his older brother, Jason Owen. Both men had been charged with torturing their own grandmother to try and force her to change her will, but the lady died of pneumonia before they could be brought to trial, and the charges were dropped. Several months after his younger brother Steven joined Connelly at her house on Penshurst Road, in the London borough of Haringey, Owen moved in with his 15 year old girlfriend and three of his children, all under five years old.

Tracey Connelly is said to have spent her days watching porn on TV, and trawling the internet, leaving her boyfriend and his brother to their own devices, amongst the snakes, dogs, and seven children in the home. At this time, both Peter and the youngest of his three sisters were on the child protection register.

§

Peter was seen by four different hospital trusts, and from 22 December 2006, he was the subject of a multi-agency child protection plan involving social services, health services and the police, whose failings and lack of inter-communication have been widely condemned. In addition, there were staff changes in all the agencies, and the family moved house at the height of his torture, leading to a lack of consistency in his care.

The timeline of events that led up to Peter's murder can seem confusing. (Perhaps in part to the incompleteness of the two serious case reviews that were produced following his death, with various dates and potentially useful pieces of information being redacted from the reports. More of these reviews later.)

The build-up to Peter's inclusion on the child protection register began three months earlier. In September 2006, Tracey Connelly took Peter to the family GP, with the common childhood complaints of a cough and nappy rash, but she was at pains to inform the doctor that her 6-month-old son, who was not yet fully mobile, bruised easily. On a further visit, a month later, the GP noted that Peter's head and chest were bruised, but accepted the explanation that he had fallen down the stairs. The doctor advised the installation of a stair-gate. At this time, Peter's father was still in frequent contact with his children, but it is believed that Tracey had now begun seeing Barker, although to what extent is unclear.

When, on 11 December 2006, the same GP, Dr Ikwueke, observed a bulge in the middle of Peter's forehead, as well as further bruising over his body, he became suspicious of Mrs Connelly's claim that she didn't know what had happened, and referred mother and baby to Dr Heather Mackinnon, a specialist at the Whittington Hospital in north London. Dr Mackinnon immediately referred Peter to Haringey children's services. The following day, at a meeting attended by a social worker and a police officer, it was agreed that Peter would not be discharged from hospital into his mother's care, and indeed, would not return home until child protection and criminal investigations had been carried out. A foster family was found, and Peter's father also offered to care for his son, but Tracey rejected both of these and was allowed to place Peter with a family friend, to whom he was discharged from hospital on 23 December.

From early January 2007, agencies involved with the family were focusing primarily on Tracey Connelly's mental health and the conditions in the family home, rather than the safety of the children.

On 26 January, despite the fact that the police investigation was not yet concluded (it was stalled for several weeks due to a changeover of staff), and enquiries about the male friend, who had by now been mentioned on a handful of occasions, had not been carried out, Peter was returned to his mother's care. The family were noted to be living in cramped and dirty conditions, and they moved to a larger home on 19 February 2007. It was still not known to the authorities that Barker was living with Connelly and her four young children.

With the criminal investigation stalled and Peter back in the family home, the first real opportunity to save him was gone.

On 9 April 2007, Peter's mother took him to the Accident and Emergency department at the North Middlesex Hospital, where she told the triage nurse that her friend, who was in the waiting room, had witnessed her baby's fall against a marble fireplace. This friend is now thought to be Steven Barker. Peter was admitted for observation, where he stayed for two days, with his mother in attendance. He was discharged home, with the view that his bruising, scratches and swellings were accidental.

The family was seen many times over the final months of Peter's life, but although suspicions were raised, the various agencies who witnessed his numerous injuries seemed to accept that he was an 'active child' who head-butted family members and pieces of furniture, tying in neatly with Tracey Connelly's description of her son as a 'clumsy child with a high pain threshold'.

In May 2007, the police became aware that the investigation begun in December had not been completed, and they re-started the case, although some of the evidence, from almost six months earlier, was no longer available.

On 1 June, a social worker made an unannounced visit to Peter's home, but accounts of what transpired are not clear. However, there was sufficient concern about the little boy's condition, and that of one of his sisters, to heighten police involvement, who subsequently arrested and bailed Tracey Connelly.

The level of support offered to Mrs Connelly was increased, with the provision of a childminder for Peter and his sister, four days per week. Regrettably, this arrangement came to an abrupt end after only a few short weeks, when other parents (understandably) complained about the Connelly children's head lice infestation.

And it still seems that none of the many services who were providing support for Tracey Connelly were aware that there were now two adult men sharing her home. Had they known, it is reasonable to suppose that they would have viewed Peter's injuries in a different light.

On 1 August, Peter's mother took him to St Ann's Clinic for his long-awaited assessment, where locum paediatrician, Sabah Al-Zayyat, ascertained that he was too poorly to undergo a full examination and failed to notice Peter's broken ribs and possibly broken back (the timing of this injury is not certain), although she did notice bruising on his face and shoulder blades.

§

Within two days of the appointment, the little boy was dead. In addition to his broken bones and bruising, Peter's fingertips were mutilated and his fingernails had been pulled out. He is believed to have died either as result of swallowing a tooth while being punched, or as a consequence of his broken back.

§

As there was an absence of forensic or other reliable evidence from those involved in Peter's last moments, a murder conviction would have been almost impossible to obtain, and therefore, in November 2008, the three defendants were instead found guilty of causing or allowing Peter's death, to which Connelly pleaded guilty.

Connelly and Barker were also tried in April 2009 on charges relating to the rape of a two year old girl who was also on the Haringey Child Protection Register. Barker was found guilty of rape, whilst Connelly was found not guilty of child cruelty.

Tracey Connelly was sentenced to be imprisoned until no longer deemed to be a risk to small children, with a minimum tariff of five years. She was released on licence in 2013 but breached her parole and was returned to prison in 2015. At the time of writing she has been refused parole three times and remains in Low Newton prison, County Durham.

Steven Barker was sentenced to life imprisonment with a minimum of 10 years for the rape, and 12 years for his part in Peter's death, both sentences to run concurrently. Barker is still behind bars.

Jason Owen's original sentence of life imprisonment with a minimum of three years was changed on appeal to a fixed six year term, and he was released on licence in August 2011. He was recalled to prison when he breached the terms of his parole, but was re-released at the end of his sentence, in 2014.

Peter's torture and murder took place in the same London Borough as that of Victoria Climbié, only seven years earlier, causing widespread condemnation of the authorities involved with the family.

§

The first Serious Case Review about Peter was deemed inadequate, and a second Review was commissioned, with both being published in October 2010. Although we know little about Peter's birth father, the Review states that he retained close involvement with his children after the separation from his wife, but was later pushed out of the picture. He had had no prior involvement with agencies, whereas Tracey appeared to use them at every turn, and knew how to 'work the system'. The latter seems to be one of the reasons that Peter's injuries were not always discovered, as she was practised in evading awkward questions. Nor were the consequences for the child's obvious injuries severe enough; for example, allowing a family friend to look after Peter when he was first removed from Tracey's care in December 2006, and the police not following up on their initial investigation before allowing him to be returned to his mother.

Blame has been apportioned to several agencies and also to particular individuals, as although there was a great deal of contact with the family, as I remarked earlier, the focus had frequently been upon supporting the mother and keeping the family together. This may often be the best policy, but tragically in this case, it proved not to be. The media, with a massive campaign by the Sun newspaper, were baying for blood, and found their scapegoats in social worker Maria Ward and Director Sharon Shoesmith. Maria Ward's caseload was 50% higher than the limit she should have been assigned, and like many others, she appears to have been reassured by Connelly's semblance of co-operation.

§

It is this reluctance of agencies, and we, the general public, to look below the surface and question what we see and hear, which prompted my ABCD mantra, which make up the subtitles of my series of books:

Assume Nothing

Be Vigilant

Check Everything

Do Something

The mistakes of the police, who failed to question Connelly under caution, did not investigate who 'Steve' was, nor ask questions of the children in the household, were glossed over. Moreover, they lost the case in the system for two months, and then said, somewhat astonishingly, that there was no case to answer on the day before Peter died.

In the December 2014 BBC documentary, 'Baby P – the untold story', the inadequacies of St Ann's hospital, a branch of the well-regarded Great Ormond Street, were exposed. The doctor who saw Peter two days before his death was found to be a locum, with no background information available to her on the patients she was treating, and with little experience in child protection. She had been appointed above her level of experience, due to the clinic being dangerously understaffed. (Much was made of the locum doctor overlooking Peter's broken back, though it was later revealed that this could have occurred *after* his appointment at St Ann's.)

Following Peter's post mortem, the hospital board ordered a report to be completed by paediatricians Professor Jonathan Sibert and Dr Deborah Hodes. However, not all the information in this report was passed on to the first serious case review panel, including the part which described St Ann's as clinically risky.

Peter's GP, Dr Ikwueke, was suspended for 18 months, despite referring the 6-month-old baby to specialist Dr Mackinnon as early as December 2006, who in turn informed children's services and the police, resulting in Peter being removed from his home, albeit only to the care of a family friend. If appropriate action had then continued, such as the police insisting on determining the true cause of Peter's injuries instead of being fobbed off with vague suggestions by his mother, Peter could have been kept safely away from the abusive environment he was now living in.

Sadly, Dr Ikwueke did not fully examine Peter in July 2007, although he noticed that the child was 'not himself'. Had he done so, he would doubtless have referred Peter once more to hospital, when one would hope that Peter would finally be safe. But we cannot be sure. After all, Peter was already on the child protection register, and his family had received 60 visits from the police, children's services, and health professionals in the previous eight months. But if any of these agencies had ascertained who was now living in the family home, we can reasonably assume that Peter would not have died.

§

Child protection services were demonised in the tabloid press, with The Sun and News of the World newspapers demanding the sacking of Sharon Shoesmith, the Director of Haringey Children's Services. Shoesmith's department had recently undergone an Ofsted inspection and been awarded a 'good' grading, which means that either the department *was* performing well, or that there were serious flaws in the inspection *process*, possibly country-wide. The Sun's campaign, led by Rebekah Brooks, amassed 1,500,000 signatures from their readers, and demanded that the Secretary of State for Children, Ed Balls, should sack Shoesmith. (Several years later, Shoesmith's sacking was found to have been unjust.) The press printed photographs of the five individuals they had in their sights, one of whom was given an apology two years later. In addition to the focus on individuals employed by children's services, the frenzy whipped up by the media led to the public hounding of a paediatrician, mistakenly believed to be a paedophile, and a number of other innocent men being 'outed' as paedophiles in their communities.

'The story of Baby P: Setting the record straight', by Ray Jones, published in 2014 by the Policy Press at the University of Bristol, catalogues the way in which the press skewed public opinion against child protection workers, whilst glossing over the fact that the police had seen Peter and his mother on the day before he died, and told her there was no evidence to press charges. Furthermore, an embarrassing outcome of the police investigation was their suggestion that the police social worker should organise a family holiday for Tracey Connelly.

The aftermath of Peter's death shows us how complex these cases can be, and how much we seem to focus on those who are trying to help children (albeit with multiple failings), deflecting the blame from those who actually tortured and killed them.

Some of the most poignant yet level-headed words about Peter were spoken by his father, and were reported in the Daily Mail on 15th November 2008, following the sentencing of his son's killers.

'I loved him deeply. I remember how, when he was in his pram, he would bounce up and down until I took him out, giving me hugs and kisses. Those who systematically tortured Peter, and killed him, kept it a secret. Not just from me, but from all the people who visited the house up until Peter's death. Even after he died, they lied to cover up their abuse. The verdicts will help to bring closure for what has been a very traumatic time for me, Peter's family, and indeed all those who knew and were close to him.'

He also had the dignity to thank everyone who had worked hard since his son's death to bring about justice, including the police and social workers who he said had acted 'with professionalism and courtesy'. The report closes with Mr Connelly thanking his family and friends for their support.

§

Some of Peter's happier moments were shared with me by his childminder, Ann Walker. By the time Peter and his sister were placed with Ann in June 2007, Connelly, Barker and Owen had been terrorising the children for a number of months. Ann remembers that Peter was quiet and rarely smiled, but that he loved to play with a big white teddy bear she had. He preferred being outside over being indoors; whether being taken to the park, or joining Ann on the school run. Perhaps he felt safer outside, as his life indoors at home was filled with fear. It is tragic that due to the Connelly children's lice infestation, Ann was only able to provide a happy respite for Peter and his sister for a few short weeks.

Ann took the iconic photograph of Peter standing on the black and white tiled floor in her kitchen. She told me that Peter loved biscuits, and that when given one of her own, his sister would snap it in half and share it with him, and that the little girl often cuddled her baby brother. That is the image of Baby P that I will treasure.

My thanks to Ann for her glimpses into Peter's life.

Rest Safely in Peace, Peter

Who Tortures Children?

Baby Peter is just one of the 3,500 children who are abused to death every year, with 2 dying every week in the UK, and 27 per week in the US.

When I first read these figures, I just couldn't believe that we are not doing more to protect them.

In general, perpetrators act alone, or in couples. Peter's case is a little more unusual, with three adults involved. The next story, that of Sylvia Likens, is rarer still, with multiple people, over a wide age range, participating in her torture.

Child murderers cover the range of caregivers, including birth parents, foster carers, grandparents, God-parents, and adoptive parents.

And fairly frequently, it is step-parents, who have an increased urge to wield power, both over their spouse, and over another man or woman's child, and take the lead in torturing their partner's offspring, sometimes with the collusion (or indifference) of the birth parent. This was the case with Tracey Connelly and Steven Barker.

Children who have been removed from their birth parents for their own safety or as a temporary measure, may find themselves in the hands of torturers. Amongst the majority of foster carers and adoptive parents who give children a loving and secure home, a minority, such as those of Sylvia Likens (in the next story), are not averse to sentencing their charges to a life of hell.

JESSICA JACKSON

Get Me Out of Here

Sylvia Marie Likens

03.01.49 - 26.10.65

aged 16 years & 9 months

Indianapolis, Indiana

When I first came across this child's story, I couldn't bear to read the details, and decided not to include it in my books. Amid the many cases of heartbreaking cruelty, this one just felt too much.

Many months later, my research into other children somehow led me back to Sylvia, when I came upon *Torture Mom* by Ryan Green, and I looked into the reasons for my hesitation. I saw that it sprang from twin sources; revulsion at the overt sexual humiliation of Sylvia, and the sickening voyeurism, both of which infest this child's tortured death. I asked myself, am I adding myself, and my readers, to the voyeurs who gathered round and participated in her degradation? Should I instead, in my own small way, afford her the dignity she was denied in the last months of her life, by steering clear? Or can I respect her life more honourably by telling her story?

I still don't know the answer.

The case shines a light into the grubbiest corners of humanity, showing how one person's whim can create a living hell for another. We see the depths of bestiality we can sink to. How we follow the herd, tentatively at first, but are soon baying for blood with the rest of the pack, partly out of fear, perhaps, that we could suddenly become the next victim.

There are several works about this case, which has been described as 'the most terrible crime ever committed in the state of Indiana', and most of my American readers will be familiar with it. Because of my conflicted feelings about Sylvia's ordeal, I have chosen to simply tell her story, rather than include my usual fictionalised element.

§

Sylvia Likens and her younger sister Jenny were two of five children born to Lester and Betty Likens. The family was poor, and when Lester and Betty managed to find work with a travelling carnival, they made the decision to entrust the care of Sylvia, aged sixteen, and Jenny, aged fifteen, to mother of seven, Gertrude Baniszewski. Mr and Mrs Likens agreed to pay the divorced home-maker $20 per week, until they could return home and collect their daughters.

The Baniszewski household was not a typical family home. Gertrude allowed her children almost unlimited freedom, and the neighbourhood kids were welcome to either rampage or lounge around the filthy house whenever they chose. Gossiping, bickering and smoking were encouraged, but Gertrude drew the line at sexual relations for her children, and imposed a bizarre semi-religious discipline upon her offspring.

Mrs Baniszewski took a dislike to the attractive and personable Sylvia from the start, and when the first pay cheque from Mr Likens didn't arrive on the agreed date, she swiftly vented her frustration on the girl and her sister. Baniszewski pulled down their underwear, and in view of the sundry visitors to her home, proceeded to use a wooden paddle on the teenage girls' buttocks. Tragically, the cheque, which had been held up in the mail, arrived a day or two later. But the abuse was already under way.

It is unclear why, after this first incident, Sylvia was selected for increasingly sadistic 'punishment'. Perhaps, with her disability due to childhood polio, her sister Jenny was less of a threat to Baniszewski's twisted sense of her own womanhood.

Gertrude was the third of six children, born into the Van Fossan family in 1928, and was singled out to be the child her father doted upon. This led to resentment from her mother, who soon isolated Gertrude, and turned her siblings against her. Her mother barely spoke to her and showed her no affection. To add to Gertrude's troubles, she had neither friends at school nor from amongst the neighbourhood kids. When her father died, his favourite daughter had no allies in the home, and when she suffered nightmares, her mother punished her for disturbing her brothers' and sisters' sleep. It is not difficult to see the similarities between Gertrude's own childhood experiences and her scapegoating of Sylvia.

When Gertrude reached puberty, her conflicted relationship with sex began to form. Though initially prudish, she realised that boys became interested in her if she touched them intimately and allowed them to touch her in return. By her mid-teens, she had gained a reputation for being 'easy' and the boys were practically queuing up for a fumble with Gertrude. The gossip about her probably grew far beyond the reality of her encounters, but it served her well when, at the age of sixteen, she successfully escaped her miserable family life by marrying for the first time. Her new husband's high expectations of a thrilling sex life soon fizzled out however, when Gertrude turned out to be an almost frigid partner when anything more than touching and kissing was involved; his outwardly promiscuous bride believed that sexual intercourse was a mortal sin.

Nevertheless, in time, the marriage produced four children, with Gertrude discovering a fierce maternal instinct that continued throughout her life; her own offspring could do no wrong. Unfortunately, her husband proved to be a violent man, and Gertrude endured ten years of beatings before divorcing John Baniszewski, and marrying for the second time. This union lasted only one year, and soon Gertrude was back with John. The couple married again, and during the seven stormy years they spent together this time, she bore him two more children. When they divorced again, Gertrude was in need of financial stability, and she found it in Dennis Wright, a man ten years her junior, who owned a large house, and who the single mother of six was able to ensnare with her sexual exploits.

Dennis was to find her irresistible throughout the course of their tempestuous relationship, and despite being on the verge of leaving her several times, he was reeled back in to endure her rowdy brood, and the alternately spotless and filthy home they all shared. When Gertrude was in hospital giving birth to their son, however, Dennis took his chance and bolted.

Whilst she still doted on her seven children, Gertrude's instability accelerated at an alarming rate, and she soon became emaciated, with her neighbours speculating that she was chronically ill. They rallied round by offering her work, such as washing, ironing and sewing, to keep her large family fed and clothed.

When Baniszewski's eldest daughter began dating, Gertrude removed the doors to all the rooms in the house so that Paula couldn't 'get up to mischief' without her mother's knowledge. She berated the teenager for being a whore and a sinner, and began to insist on the children attending church, filling the time in between with lectures on sin and damnation. However, Paula's brief affair with a married man was carried out in secret, and she found herself pregnant. When Gertrude found out, she was in denial about the pregnancy, but her slovenliness increased, and her vindictive behaviour spiralled out of control, whilst Paula attempted to keep her pregnancy secret from her friends and other members of the family.

It was around this time that the two teenage lodgers, Sylvia and Jenny Likens, were added to the chaotic and bewildering household, and within a week they were being beaten because of the delayed payment. If the two sisters had hoped they would escape further punishments now that the money had been received, they were gravely mistaken.

In common with many children of the 1960's, Sylvia collected empty lemonade bottles which she returned to the store in return for a little cash, with which she proceeded to buy sweets for herself and the Baniszewski children. But Gertrude reacted with insane fury, accusing her of stealing the sweets. She once again beat Sylvia mercilessly, screaming abuse at her, and revelling in the girl's terror and confusion.

The Likens girls quickly learnt that it was wise to keep out of Mrs Baniszewski's way.

§

Life for Sylvia so far had not been especially easy as the middle child (she was born between two sets of twins) of the Likens family. Her parents struggled to make ends meet, and the children were occasionally boarded out with family or friends. But we can hope that Sylvia had known at least some degree of love and affection, and for the first few weeks at the Baniszewski house, she retained her bright and cheerful outlook. Sylvia had always loved roller skating (helping her disabled sister around the rink), dancing, and listening to the Beatles. She was naturally pretty, and like most teenage girls, in her shy way, she enjoyed the attention she got from boys.

Sylvia and Jenny soon found that food was scarce in their new home and when the local preacher, Reverend Julian, gave the girls some tiny sandwiches and a small chocolate cake at an after-school function, they tried not to cram the food down as ravenously as they wanted to. On their return home, after Sylvia had seen Jenny safely into bed, she nervously ventured into the lounge, only to find that the other children were laughing at her and calling her 'piggy'.

Then Gertrude reared up from her chair and screamed at Sylvia that she'd brought disgrace upon her family by her disgusting greed, and that if she was so hungry then she had something for her to eat. The woman searched the almost bare cupboards, and finding a hotdog sausage, she rammed it into a bun and smothered it in so much ketchup and mustard that it was dripping off the dirty table and onto the kitchen floor. Despite Sylvia's protests, Gertrude shoved the food into her mouth, right to the back of her throat, and the girl was forced to chew. With eyes and nose streaming, Sylvia choked and threw up onto the floor. This incensed Baniszewski, who pushed her down to her knees, placed her foot on her back, and ranted at her until she'd eaten the vomit, while the other children gathered round and laughed.

§

During a short visit back to Indianapolis, Sylvia's parents were keen to see their daughters, and Gertrude arranged that they should all meet away from the filthy house, lest they see the awful conditions the girls were living in. Throughout the meeting, Gertrude held Sylvia in check with warning glares, and explained that the girls' weight loss was due to supporting her own daughter on her slimming diet. She praised their helping out at the church, and once when Sylvia seemed on the verge of tears, Gertrude managed to find a way of explaining that away too. A chance for the Likens girls to be saved was gone.

During the next few weeks, Gertrude showed that she was pleased they hadn't told their parents about their treatment, by being slightly kinder to Sylvia and Jenny. Even the eldest daughters of the family, Paula and Stephanie, were friendlier, and warily at first, the Likens sisters were drawn into the group of teenagers who gossiped and joked in the Baniszewski lounge. When the talk turned to boys and boyfriends, 16 year old Sylvia eventually confided that she had kissed a boy and had once allowed him to touch her on the outside of her jumper. The boys in the room cheered and the girls smiled. Gertrude, however, was incensed, and yelled that Sylvia was a whore and a prostitute. From that moment, Sylvia Marie Likens was doomed. In a tirade against the girl, Gertrude kicked her repeatedly in the crotch, and accused her of bringing shame on her family by becoming pregnant (which of course, she wasn't). She enlisted the help of the boys to hold Sylvia's legs apart, the better to stomp on her, as she ranted at the girl, and encouraged all the children present to hate all whores, like Sylvia.

Paula and Stephanie Baniszewski took their cruelty to Sylvia into the schoolroom, making her reviled wherever she went. Unfortunately for Sylvia, this coincided with a rumour circulating that Paula was pregnant (which indeed, she was) and that the Baniszewski girls were being paid for having sex. This rumour was picked up by Stephanie's boyfriend, Coy Hubbard, who raced to Gertrude's house, and accused Sylvia of spreading the rumour, saying she should be taught a lesson. Stephanie and Coy raved at Sylvia, saying it was she who was the whore, and Gertrude egged Coy on to hit her. When that wasn't quite enough for her tormentors, Coy was encouraged to perform his judo moves on Sylvia, and he began throwing her around the room. Still not satisfied, Gertrude had Coy drag her by the hair, down into the basement, where he could toss her against the walls as Gertrude watched from the stairs.

When he had finished, Sylvia was left, battered and bruised, to spend the night alone in the basement, while Gertrude told Coy he should come and practise his moves on her lodger as often as he was able.

Baniszewski continued to ensure that Sylvia was isolated, by telling the few friends the girl had left that she had been spreading lies about themselves and their families. Even her teachers at school seemed willing to believe that Sylvia deserved the bruises on her body; that she was a nasty and untrustworthy child. Gertrude even forced Jenny to hit her sister. Being kept without adequate clothing as the days grew colder, in desperation for a little warmth, Sylvia stole a tracksuit from a school-mate's locker, and was once again branded a thief, a liar and a prostitute. Gertrude kicked the girl in her crotch, grinding her heel as hard as she could, while Sylvia screamed in agony. Then, relishing a new form of punishment, Gertrude held her lit cigarette against each of her fingers in turn. And in the living room filled with teenagers, she humiliated Sylvia by beating her bare buttocks with a belt, before inviting them all to put out their cigarettes on Sylvia's skin.

Sylvia was starving, exhausted, and crippled with the fear of what might happen next. One evening, desperate to eat, she raised enough money, by returning empty bottles, to buy herself a meal. Gertrude flew at her on her return, dragging her into the crowded living room, and accused her of walking the streets, selling her body. The woman forced Sylvia to strip naked for the boys gathered there, and then push an empty cola bottle into her vagina. When she couldn't push it in far enough to satisfy Gertrude, the latter shoved it roughly in. Sylvia bled onto the floor and passed out with the pain.

In mid-September, the father of one of the local boys phoned the school Sylvia had been attending, to report that one of their pupils had open sores over most of her body. As she had not been in attendance recently, the school nurse visited the Baniszewski home, to be told by Gertrude that the girl had run away the previous week. She claimed that Sylvia had been a bad influence on all the children in her care, and that the sores on her body were due to her lack of personal hygiene. The school made no further attempts to trace Sylvia.

§

From that moment on, the helpless girl was kept naked, starving and cold in the filthy basement. When she had no choice but to wet herself, her captor roared at her for being unclean, and invented a new 'punishment'. Boiling the water on the stove, a scalding bath was prepared, and several eager children bound Sylvia hand and foot and immersed her in the water, rubbing her skin with salt to heighten her agony. Although initially hesitant, a 14 year old boy named Ricky Hobbs, who was in thrall of Gertrude, was recruited to join in this and future tortures. The scalding bath became part of Sylvia's daily routine, causing large patches of skin to peel from her body, along with being forced to eat her own faeces and drink her own urine. Paula took delight in choking and punching Sylvia, and throwing hot water in her face. On one occasion she punched Sylvia so hard, concentrating the blows on her teeth and eyes, that Paula broke her own wrist. When her injury was placed in a plaster cast, Paula simply used it to beat Sylvia further.

All the children seemed to relish the regular pastime of pushing Sylvia down the cellar stairs, watching her head and body crash against the walls and steps as she tumbled helplessly down.

The Baniszewski family also devised a money-making scheme, whereby for a few cents, kids could come along and watch, or even participate in, Sylvia's torture and humiliation.

§

After a few weeks, Gertrude offered Sylvia a ray of hope, saying that if she could spend the night in the upstairs bedroom without wetting herself, she would not be returned to the dank basement. Gertrude's son John, daughter Stephanie, and the ever-present Coy Hubbard, duly tied their victim to the bed. Unfortunately for Sylvia, her treatment at the hands of her tormentors had rendered her incontinent, and she was unable to comply with

Gertrude's orders. She must have been terrified when she realised that she had wet the bed. Gertrude seemed to wonder what more she could do to hurt Sylvia. First she put an old dress on her, so that she could humiliate the teenager by making her strip in front of the boys, and once again be made to force a cola bottle into her vagina. Then, accusing Sylvia of branding her daughters as prostitutes, Gertrude screamed that she was going to brand her. With a gag pushed into her mouth, and held down by a few of the boys, the 16 year old girl, now little more than a skeleton, watched in helpless terror as Gertrude heated a needle in the flame of a match and began to carve out a phrase on her stomach. 'I'M A PROSTITUTE AND PROUD OF IT'. When Gertrude began to tire, the sadistic task was completed by children as young as ten. Ricky Hobbs hit Sylvia several times. Her crime? She had flinched as he was branding her. Sylvia's ordeal was not quite over, with Coy dragging her down to the basement, and once again hurling the wretched girl against its walls.

The following night, Gertrude came down to the cellar and hauled Sylvia upstairs, throwing her onto a bed, where she was left to sleep for several hours, before being immersed in the bath; this time one of a comfortable temperature. Did Sylvia hope that her torture was over? That the woman and her cruel brood had come to their senses? Or that the last few months had been a ghastly nightmare? Baniszewski and her two eldest daughters dressed Sylvia in a summer dress and sat her up at the dining table. They put a piece of paper in front of her and a pen in her hand. Then they instructed her to write. And she obediently grasped the pen as strongly as she could and began to write her own death sentence.

To Mr and Mrs Likens:

I went with a gang of boys in the middle of the night. And they said that they would pay me if I would give them something so I got in the car and they all got what they wanted ... and when they got finished they beat me up and left sores on my face and all over my body. And they also put on my stomach, I am a prostitute and proud of it.

I have done just about everything that I could do just to make Gertie mad and cost Gertie more money than she's got. I've tore up a new mattress and peed on it. I have also cost Gertie doctor bills that she really can't pay and made Gertie a nervous wreck and all the kids ...

The letter gave Gertrude Baniszewski the evidence she felt she might need if questions were asked about the physical condition of her 16 year old lodger, should she be found, alive or dead. She discussed with Paula her plan to dump Sylvia at the local refuse site and leave her there to die. Their captive must have overheard, as she tried to make a break for it. But she was far too weak to get further than the hallway, where she was stopped in her tracks and dragged back into the kitchen. Gertrude was surprisingly gentle, offering her some toast to eat. Sylvia gratefully tried to eat the dry bread, but couldn't get the food down her throat. Baniszewski obliged by ramming a curtain rod into Sylvia's mouth, smashing the metal pole against her teeth, and ordering the girl be returned to the basement, where Gertrude proceeded to punch her repeatedly in the stomach. The following day, Coy took up the curtain rod and beat the almost lifeless girl again and again and again.

In the dead of night, Sylvia regained consciousness and searched in the darkness for anything that could help her. She dragged herself across the dirt floor and summoned all the power she had left to carry the head of a spade, and bang it as hard as she could against the wall. The neighbours whose sleep she disturbed did nothing, and when her strength failed, she slumped helplessly to the ground.

§

Sylvia's nightmare was not quite over. On the morning of 26 October, unable to speak intelligibly nor co-ordinate her movements, the girl was dragged up from the basement and offered food. When she was unable to eat it, Gertrude Baniszewksi threw her to the ground. Returned to the basement in a state of shock, Sylvia was viewed by an assortment of her tormentors as her body jerked and she spoke incoherently. She was sprayed with a garden hose in a feeble attempt to wash her clean, and even in her weakened state, Sylvia made one last attempt to escape. Gertrude allegedly stamped on her head, and soon after, Sylvia was dead.

It was now time for the Baniszewskis put their flimsy plan into action. The police were phoned and Sylvia was reported missing, and when they arrived, Gertrude repeated her belief that a prostitute like that was sure to come to grief, and showed the perplexed officers the bizarre letter of confession. As they made to leave without discovering what had actually happened to her sister, Jenny Likens took her chance, whispering, 'Get me out of here, and I'll tell you everything.'

To Jenny's relief, one of the policemen turned back towards Gertrude and the children, as if he had just made his mind up to follow procedure after all. 'We need to question everyone.' He pointed to Jenny. 'We'll start with you.'

§

Sylvia's autopsy revealed that she had suffered between 150 and 200 separate wounds in various stages of healing. These included burns, severe bruising, extensive muscle and nerve damage, and peeling of most of the layers of skin upon her face, breasts, neck, and right knee.

Her vagina was almost swollen shut, and her hymen was intact, making it more likely that Sylvia was a virgin than the pregnant prostitute Baniszewski had accused her of being. During her dying hours, the agonised girl had bitten her bottom lip to shreds, severing it from her face in several places. Her fingernails were broken backwards, either from another form of torture, or from her own vain attempts to claw her way to freedom.

The cause of Sylvia's death was brain swelling, internal haemorrhaging of the brain, shock resulting from the extensive skin damage, and severe malnutrition.

§

Much has been written about the Likens sisters' apparent reluctance to call for help. Perhaps growing up in a family of five children where money was scarce, and being boarded out fairly often, taught the girls to simply accept whatever came their way. Perhaps their own birth parents were so preoccupied with struggling to find work and keeping their stormy marriage afloat, that the kids sometimes weren't listened to when they raised concerns. Sylvia and Jenny certainly lived through a time (the 1950's and early 1960's), when abuse of children was not the hot topic it is today, and they wouldn't have been aware of any agencies they might've been able to turn to. There was a culture of children being seen and not heard, and adults knowing best, and corporal punishment was rife both at home and at school.

The Baniszewski household fabricated such rumours about Sylvia that many adults who could've helped her, such as teachers, neighbours, and parents of their classmates, instead colluded with the story that Sylvia was a lying whore who could not be trusted and deserved to be punished.

When the torture was escalating, Jenny had called on their sister Dianna for help, but the older girl initially thought her sibling was exaggerating their situation in order to leave the Baniszewski's and make their home with Dianna and her young family. When she did pay a visit to her sisters, Gertrude met her at the door, and would not let her into the house, which raised Dianna's suspicions, and she contacted social services. When a worker visited the home, a terrified Jenny told her that everything was fine, but that Sylvia had run away, which seemed to satisfy the authorities. Jenny lived under the constant threat of receiving the same torture as her sister if she told outsiders what was going on.

Paula Baniszewski gave birth to a daughter in January 1966, who she named Gertrude, in honour of her mother.

In May 1966, at a joint trial of Gertrude and her eldest daughter, Paula, the most compelling evidence was given by Jenny Likens, and 11 year old Marie Baniszewski. Gertrude Baniszewski was found guilty of first-degree murder, while Paula Baniszewski was found guilty of second-degree murder. They were sentenced to life imprisonment at the Indiana Women's Prison.

Fifteen year old Stephanie was also indicted for first-degree murder, but she agreed to turn state's evidence and the charges against her were dropped.

Ricky Hobbs, John Baniszewski, and Coy Hubbard were convicted of manslaughter. For their part in Sylvia's torture and death, they each served a two year sentence at the Indiana State Reformatory in Pendleton. Richard Hobbs died of cancer in 1972. John Baniszewski changed his name to John Blake, and he died in 2005. He was the only perpetrator to show public remorse for Sylvia's torture and murder. Coy Hubbard remained in the Indianapolis area all his life, and died in 2007.

Four or five neighbourhood children, amongst the many who had abused Sylvia physically, mentally and emotionally, were initially charged with injury-to-person, but these charges were later dropped.

In 1971, the Indiana Supreme Court granted Gertrude and Paula Baniszewski new separate trials due to a 'prejudicial atmosphere' during their previous joint trial. The outcome for Gertrude was to again be convicted of first-degree murder, while Paula pleaded guilty to a lesser charge of voluntary manslaughter and served about another two years in prison, making a total of seven years. As Paula Pace, she moved to Iowa where she worked for fourteen years as a teacher's aide, before being fired when it was discovered that she had lied on her application. She is the only one of the five convicted who is alive today.

Gertrude Baniszewski also relocated to Iowa, after being paroled in 1985 amid a public outcry. She died of lung cancer in 1990.

§

Although Sylvia's death occurred so many years ago, before many of us were born, most American citizens are aware of her horrific death. In 2001, a memorial was dedicated to Sylvia in Willard Park, Indianapolis. Several hundred people attended the ceremony. And in Lebanon, Boone County, 'Sylvia's Child Advocacy Center' strives to support abused children and prevent further deaths. In addition, allegedly prompted by the fact that neighbours were aware of Sylvia's suffering but did not act to help her, all citizens of Indiana are legally mandated to report their suspicions of child abuse to the authorities.

§

I have made the decision not to show photographs of the children when ravaged by their injuries and death, but instead show how they were in life; where possible, before the worst of the torture began. When I look at the photograph of Sylvia at the beginning of this chapter, I see an attractive, healthy teenager on the brink of all that life had to offer. There is a serenity about her, and a quiet confidence that all would be well.

But if you find the photographs of Sylvia's corpse on the internet, perhaps you, like me, will look with horror at her mutilated body, and shed a tear for her the next time someone trots out the platitude, 'Everything happens for a reason'.

Rest Safely in Peace, Sylvia

The Abuser's Childhood

Perpetrators of child murder often grow up in households where they are not shown love, or, like Gertrude Baniszewski, are subjected to a warped version of it. A child naturally seeks to love and be loved by their parents, but this if is consistently denied, and they are instead subjected to significant, relentless abuse, they may grow up without the capacity to love and care for their own children.

As a child, Gertrude Baniszewski's experience of love was certainly confusing; adored by her father, and vilified by her mother and her siblings.

As an adult, she passed on this chaotic form of parental love to her own children and those in her care. Her experience as a battered spouse further compounded these problems, and once she held Sylvia and Jenny in her power, and had her violence endorsed by the likes of Coy Hubbard and Ricky Hobbs, the stage was set.

Thankfully, not every child who grows up in an abusive home becomes an abuser. Within the same family, each child's own experience will vary, even when appearing similar on the surface.

I believe that a child who never experiences love, encouragement, or someone who believes in them, may grow up without the capacity to love and care for their own children. It is also my feeling that *without* a history of some form of violence or neglect, it would be rare for a parent to maltreat their child to death.

> I greatly admire the many abused children who break the cycle, and grow up to be nurturing parents.

A Family Christmas

'Isn't this fantastic!' I shout to my little sister above the roar of the engines.

Alex nods, braids swinging as she humps her new holdall up the metal steps. I hand the card to the stewardess.

'Five of you?' she says, returning it to me with a neatly manicured hand. 'And you're in charge?'

I nod. 'Yeah, I'm taking care of them.'

Although at twenty-two, Paul is the oldest, his autism makes people defer to my older sister Keisha or me. I like it best when it's me.

The stewardess smiles, gesturing to our seats at the front of the plane. 'Can you get the bags up into the lockers? You're nice and tall.'

'Yes, I can manage, Miss.'

The two younger ones nudge each other. 'I can manage, Miss,' they snigger in unison.

'Hey, you two! Remember what Maman and Papa said?'

My brother Thierry sighs. 'Yes, we remember, Kris. Behave yourselves, and mind your big brothers and sisters.'

Paul leans across and high fives me, and repeats what he's been saying for the past month. 'You got me something good?'

''Course I have, bro.'

'Did you remember what I wanted?'

'Yeah, don't you worry about that.'

And he high fives me again.

Our small cases hold more presents than clothes, and although I'm too grown up to admit it to Paul and the rest of my siblings, like them, I can't wait till Christmas morning.

When we're all seated, the stewardess comes back and makes sure we're clipped into our seat-belts. 'I'm Trudi,' she says. 'Just press this button if you need anything. I'll be round with the comics once we're in the air.' She must've seen the look on my face, because she adds, 'For the little ones.'

I crane my neck right round to watch Trudi sashay towards the back of the cabin, and grab my jumper to cover my groin. I blush and grin to myself; who'd be a teenage boy!

Keisha is nodding against my shoulder, and the others are engrossed in their magazines and comics when Trudi comes back and crouches down beside me. 'So, going away for Christmas?'

'Yes. We're going to spend the holiday with my sister in London.'

'That sounds like fun. You must be so excited.'

'The kids can't wait,' I say, hoping to sound sophisticated. 'And I'm looking forward to seeing my brother-in-law. We'll probably go out to the pub together while the children are playing.' Thierry would go crazy if he heard me; he's only two years younger than me.

Trudi has the loveliest smile. There's just a hint of red lipstick coating a front tooth. 'Won't your parents miss you? Especially at Christmas?'

'Yes, they will.' I swallow hard. I'll miss them too. 'But they're coming to join us for the new year.'

'What do you do, back home? Do you live in Paris?'

'Yes, we do.' I pause for a second. 'And I'll be going into business soon.'

Trudi looks impressed. She doesn't need to know I'm only fifteen and still at school. I imagine my mother scolding me for fibbing, but I *will* soon be joining my father in his carpentry business.

'A hard-working man, then? You'll make a fine catch one day.'

I sit up a little straighter. 'My brother-in-law's a football coach in London. I'll be helping him run the team while we're there.'

'Well,' she says, patting my arm, sending a thrill through my body. 'You have a great holiday, Kristy. Maybe I'll see you on your way back.'

We've seen snow at home in Paris of course, but none of us has thought to bring suitable shoes, and we're sliding all over the place on our way from the Tube to Magalie and Eric's flat in Forest Gate. After our day's travelling, by the time we get up to their place on the eighth floor, we're all feeling pretty tired.

'Oh, where's the Christmas tree?' says Alex.

That starts Paul off on one of his chants, 'No tree. No tree.'

'Come on, guys,' I say, glancing at Magalie. 'There's not enough space for a tree, but we'll still have a great Christmas.' I'm more concerned about where we're all going to sleep.

'No tree. No tree.'

'Paul, hey. Come on, now. Eric and Mag are going to think we're ungrateful.'

Magalie is bustling about making us a pot of coffee and Eric is standing looking out of the window into the darkness.

I try to catch his eye. 'So hey, Eric. How's the football going?'

He turns to look at me. 'Pretty well, Kristy. Pretty well.'

'I still play a lot, Eric. I've been getting the team into shape after you gave me those great ideas.'

'Good. That's good.'

'He's got me a great present,' says Paul. 'Haven't you, Kris?'

I smile at Eric, and roll my eyes, just a bit. 'Yes, Paul. You'll like it. But don't keep asking me about it.'

'I've got you something good, Kris. Bet you can't guess what it is.'

'Bet I can.'

'So, you know what present he's got you, do you Kris?' says Eric.

I smile and speak quietly, so as not to hurt my brother's feelings. 'It's not hard to know what Paul has got us.'

'Really?' Eric jabs his finger into my chest. 'I wonder how you know that, Kristy? Can you read his mind?'

'No, it's just, well, he can't keep a secret.'

Everyone has gone quiet, but I can hear Paul muttering. 'It's okay. It's okay. It's okay.'

Eric shrugs his shoulders and starts to head for the kitchen. 'Let's have that coffee, Magalie. These kids must be dying for a drink.'

But as he looks back over his shoulder at me, he reminds me of someone. I shudder as I realise it's Michael Jackson from the Thriller video. I love MJ, but the way Eric's eyes are glittering at me is more than a bit weird. It's frightening.

Somehow, we've all managed to squash onto the black vinyl sofa and chairs, and we're slurping our coffee and dunking chunks of bread into it.

Eric is roaming round the flat, checking the windows and doors. When he finally comes to join us, he's tapping a wooden stick, a bit like a baseball bat, against the palm of his hand.

'Y'know,' he says when he finally stops pacing. 'There's a lot of witchcraft all over the world.'

I raise my eyebrows, but say nothing.

'Oh,' says Keisha. 'I didn't know that.'

'Well, there is, girl,' says Magalie. 'In Paris, in London, in the Congo.'

My ears prick up. I'm always interested to hear about the place Maman and Papa were born.

'Over there,' says Eric. 'It's called kindoki.'

I've heard of that. 'That's a kind of possession by spirits, isn't it Eric?'

'Yes, yes it is, Kristy. You hear that, Mag? Kristy seems to know a lot about kindoki.'

'Well, not really. I've just heard the word, that's all.'

'Maybe you've heard that there are witches everywhere. Putting spells on their brothers and sisters.'

I laugh. 'Oh Eric, Magalie wouldn't do that to us.'

'Maybe I didn't mean Magalie,' he spits. You have brothers and sisters, don't you, Kris?'

I don't really understand what he means, so I shrug and let my mind wander over to Trudi, and whether she'll be there on the flight home, in her white blouse and tight skirt.

When we finally go to bed, we're crammed together really tightly, and when I get up to use the toilet, both of my brothers grunt and slap at my retreating legs. I stand in the hallway, shivering, before I remember which door I need for the bathroom. When I crawl back under the thin duvet, I'm glad of the familiar warmth of my brothers' bodies.

After breakfast, we ring home, and I feel a little put out to hear Eric call my father 'Papa'. I know Papa thinks highly of my sister's partner, but it doesn't feel right. We each take a turn to chat to Maman and Papa and promise to ring again on Christmas Day.

'Ooh,' says Thierry, peering behind the blackout curtains. 'It's snowing again. Are we going out?'

'It's too wet and cold,' says Magalie. 'We'll just stay in and talk and play games.'

I search in the sideboard for a pack of cards.

'What are you doing?' says Eric.

When I tell him he glares at me.

'Cards,' he says to Magalie. 'Your brother is looking for the devil's game.' His expression stops the laugh that is rising in my throat. He doesn't seem to be joking. But soon the shadow passes and he pulls out a game of Ludo. A game for kids. Still, we have fun; teasing Alex when she loses, then making her smile again when we let her win the next game.

After a few games, Keisha and Alex help Magalie to make toast for lunch, and I hear them laughing in the kitchen.

But Eric seems to be observing us boys, like animals in a zoo. 'Why don't you smile like your brothers?' he says to Paul.

My elder brother looks to me for an answer.

'It's his autism, Eric. He's enjoying himself, but he doesn't show it. Maman and Papa say he's different. He's special.'

'I wasn't asking you, Kristy.'

'Sorry, Eric. But I don't think Paul can answer you, brother.'

Eric looks meaningfully at Magalie as she and Keisha carry the plates of food into the lounge.

'So, you speak for him, do you?'

'Well, I … yes sometimes, if he wants me to.'

'He's controlling him, Mag. Do you see now?'

My sister nods slowly.

That night, it feels like I've just managed to get to sleep when I wake up, desperate for the toilet. I try to get up more quietly this time. I don't want to disturb Paul again; he's looking grey and tired after a day of Eric's scrutiny.

I creep to the door. Thierry stirs and turns over. I'll have to shove him across the bed to get back in again. I stand in the hallway and cross my legs. Oh no! It's too late. I feel the seeping warmth trickling into my underpants and hobble to the toilet to finish what I've started. Still half asleep, I whip off my wet pants, pull my pyjamas back up, and go and throw the underpants behind the bin in the kitchen. I can rinse them in the morning. No-one needs to know.

Eric wakes the boys early, and he and Magalie call the three of us into the kitchen. To my shame, my brother-in-law is holding my wet pants in his hand.

'What is this?'

None of us speaks.

'I ask you again, what is this?'

I know that neither Paul nor Thierry will say a word. Why should they? It's not their dirty pants being swung around like a guilty secret. But I'm scared. I don't know what Eric will do.

'Somebody is responsible for these, and I will get it out of you.'

As we stand there, I have the awful feeling I'm going to soil myself again.

'Who is it?' Before I realise what's happening, Eric has grabbed his wooden club and is beating it against Paul's shoulder. I lunge towards him as he does the same to Thierry.

'Eric, stop!'

He turns to me. 'Yes, Kristy?'

'It was me. I had an accident during the night. I was going to wash them this morning.'

'An accident!' He looks at Magalie. 'That's very interesting.' He grabs a metal bar from its place in the corner. The kind you put dumbbells on for lifting weights. In a flash, he smashes it over each of our heads.

Neither of the others make a sound. But I scream out in pain.

'They are probably innocent,' says Eric, with a nod to my brothers. Then he turns to me. 'But we may have found the witch amongst us.'

Alex and Keisha have been dragged out of bed, and all five of us have been made to assemble in the living room.

'So, you have come here to kill us,' says Eric calmly.

I catch my breath, trying to make sense of my brother-in-law's words.

'Are they all witches, Magalie? What do you think, hmm? Or maybe it's just one of them.' He looks up and down the line. 'Which of your brothers and sisters has brought kindoki into our home, Mag? Let us make sure we find the right one.'

My eyes shoot to the front door. It is loaded with locks and bolts.

'Is it you, Paul?'

I rush to protect him. 'No, Eric. Please. Paul is not a witch. None of us are.'

'I am coming to you, Kristy.' He spits out my name. 'Wait your turn.' He peers into the face of my little brother. 'Are you a witch?'

Thierry looks to me for guidance, and I shake my head. Trembling, and with eyes bulging, he does the same.

'Ah,' says Eric. He has picked up the wooden club again. 'I see you look to your leader.'

Thierry drops his gaze to the floor.

'So, Keisha. What about you? Hmm, is it you?'

Keisha does not look at me. 'I am not a witch, Eric. We don't understand why …'

Thwack. He swings the stick at her head and she screams. 'Be quiet, Witch.' He turns to my little sister. 'And what about you, Alex? Are you a witch, like Keisha?'

'No, Eric.'

Magalie calmly starts clearing away the cups and plates from yesterday evening.

I touch her elbow as she passes me. 'Mag, what's happening?'

She jerks her arm away as if I have burned her. 'Don't touch me, Witch.'

Eric whips round. Again his eyes are hard and glinting as he swings the bat and beats me on my chest. 'Are you, Kristy? Are you a witch?'

We spend the cold winter's day, and into the night, in fear, as Eric asks each one of us again and again and again if we are witches. At some point in the darkness, he decides that my two brothers are not witches, and Magalie takes them into the bedroom and ties them up with dressing gown cords and belts.

'So Kristy, so girls. It all comes down to you.'

Magalie interrupts him. 'Eric, you must sleep now.'

He glares at her but goes into the bedroom and I hear my brothers whimpering. Then all is quiet.

'Magalie,' whispers Keisha. 'Why are you calling us witches? You know we are not.'

'Shut up, Witch. Eric knows how to deal with you.'

'I'm thirsty,' says Alex.

'Nothing to eat or drink,' snaps Magalie. 'And no sleep. We need to get the kindoki out of you.'

We huddle together on the sofa for hours, prodded by our big sister whenever one of us starts to fall asleep. Although I'm exhausted, I frantically try and think what to do, and decide that if we all stay calm and do what they say, they won't hurt us any more. And anyway, Eric may have forgotten his crazy ideas by the morning. Besides, Maman and Papa will be here in a couple of days.

As the cold light trickles in at the edges of the blackout curtains, we hear stirring from the bedroom. Then Eric bursts into the room and, without saying a word, he beats the three of us with the metal pole. The pain in my head and chest is agonising, but I try to protect Alex with my body.

'Witch!' shouts Eric. 'What are you doing to your sister?'

Blood oozes from the top of my head, and when I try to wipe it from my eyes, Eric cracks the bar across my hand and I feel my fingers break. I scream.

'Be quiet, Witch,' he shouts into my face. The last thing I feel before I pass out is the metal bar smashing against my mouth and teeth falling down my throat.

When I come round, Eric is slapping the faces of my two sisters in turn.

'Are you a witch?'

'No.'

Slap. 'Are you a witch?'

'Yes.'

Slap. 'Are you a witch?'

'No. Yes. I don't know.'

Slap. 'Are you a witch?'

'Yes.'

Slap. 'Are you or aren't you a witch?'

Keisha wipes the blood from her cheek, and looks left and right in despair. 'I don't know!'

'She doesn't know, Mag. What do you think of that? The witch doesn't know. You see Keisha, if you admit it, we can drive the demon out of you.'

Keisha tries to follow his logic.

'So, are you a witch?'

'Yes, yes I am.'

'Are you?'

'Yes, Eric.'

'Are you sure?'

'Yes.'

'Say it then.'

Keisha pauses.

Slap. 'Say it, Witch. Say it.'

'I'm a witch.'

'Are you a witch? Say it!'

'I am a witch.'

'Good. We have found you out. Now we can deliver you.'

Eric is on the phone. 'Hi, Papa. Yes, we are all fine. How is Christmas Day in Paris?' A pause. Then, 'Yes, of course we're having fun. We've been playing games inside. It's too cold to go out. Oh, here's Magalie.'

'Hi, Papa. We're all looking forward to seeing you soon. How's Maman?'

'Magalie, let me speak to Papa,' I whisper.

She turns her back on me. 'Yes, I am making a big Christmas dinner later. The kids are going to help me.'

'Put me back on, Mag,' says Eric. 'They're okay. Yes, you can speak to them in a minute. But listen Papa, we've had to sort out a few little problems.' He looks directly at me. 'I have one problem in particular. Did you know that Kristy is a witch?'

I'm sure I hear my papa laugh.

'No, I'm serious. In fact, I think you need to come and pick up the children. You've definitely got to pick up Kris because he's a witch. If you don't, I'm going to kill him.'

I can't make out my papa's words, but I sense the alarm and confusion in his voice.

'I'll put Kristy on.'

I'm so dazed I can hardly hold the phone. 'Papa, come and get me. Otherwise Eric will kill me.'

Magalie grabs the handset. 'They're just joking, Papa. Yeah, we're all fine.'

I can still hear Papa's raised voice.

'No, Papa,' says Magalie. 'It's just a game we've been playing.'

Papa doesn't seem to be giving up so easily, and Magalie is losing patience.

'I promise, Papa. It's just the kids messing around. Just forget about it. What time does your flight get in on Wednesday?'

'Mag, go and untie your brothers and bring them here.'

They stagger in, looking terrified. Paul is muttering something about Christmas presents.

'Now then, boys. I need your help,' says Eric. 'The girls have admitted they're witches, so we have to beat the demons out.' He pushes sticks into their hands and commands the boys to beat Keisha and Alex.

I try to sit up, thinking I can stop them, but Magalie picks up a hammer and strikes me on the shoulder, and I slump back onto the sofa. 'Watch, Kris,' she hisses. 'It's your turn next.'

Alex is on her knees begging forgiveness, while Eric and my brothers beat her and Keisha until they fall unconscious, and finally Eric cries out. 'It is done. They are delivered.' He orders Magalie to wipe the blood from their wounds and douse them in cold water to revive them.

Then he turns to me. 'Now for the real witch amongst us. The one who came here to kill us.'

If I had some small hope of him regaining his sanity before, I lose it completely now, as I listen with horror as Eric gives his proof that I am a witch.

'We have seen how you control your brothers and sisters with your sorcery. And who but a witch would wet themselves during the night!' He licks his lips before continuing. 'You! You, Kristy, have made Paul different to everyone else, and none of you will be permitted to eat, drink or sleep until Paul is made right again. Kristy, get ready. We have many ways to drive the evil out!'

I am barely conscious of Eric appearing with a kitchen knife but I scream with each stab of the blade into my chest, as my torturer screeches, 'Cut it out, cut the evil out.'

Somehow I manage to croak at him. 'I'm not a witch, Eric.'

'See how he lies!'

Keisha crawls to my side. 'Say you are, Kris. He will punish you, but then it will end.'

'Eric, I confess. I am a witch. Please deliver me.'

My brother-in-law narrows his eyes. 'Demon! Come out of this boy! Hold him, Magalie. The rest of his teeth must go. They are keeping the devil locked inside him.' And he places the chisel against my mouth and slams down with the hammer. I howl in agony, and the hammer falls again, my teeth shooting onto the sofa. I pass out again to the sound of Paul, Keisha, Thierry and Alex screaming.

'Paul, go and bring the tiles stacked in the corner of the bedroom.'

Paul looks around him in terror, then stumbles out. He calls from the bedroom. 'They're heavy, Eric. I can't lift them.'

'One at a time, you idiot.'

My brother staggers back into the living room.

'Put it there and bring the next one.'

I catch the horrified looks on my brothers' faces as Eric orders them to hold me down, while he smashes the first tile onto my head.

The pain is unbearable. I don't know how I will endure this. 'I'm sorry, Eric. Forgive me, please.' I'm not even sure what I'm saying, or what he wants me to say. Another tile crashes onto my skull.

Thierry's eyes are streaming as he whispers, 'I'm sorry, Kris. I'm sorry.'

'Make him stop, Magalie,' screams Keisha, pulling on Eric's arm in desperation. He picks up the stick to beat her and she falls back, as he turns to me again.

After the next few blows, I start to drift in and out of consciousness. I can't tell if my eyes are open or shut. I only know that I can no longer see anything and the sounds in the room keep growing then fading, like trying to find a signal on an old radio.

'It's working,' I hear Eric say. 'The evil is leaving him.'

Perhaps it's over. Perhaps he's going to stop. He'll take us to the airport, and Maman and Papa will meet us and hug us. And I'll finish school and become a carpenter, and everyone will be proud of me and …

'He's got me a good present,' says Paul. 'Stop hurting him.'

'Not yet, fool. This is just the beginning of his deliverance.'

I'm writhing on the floor, awash with blood, sweat, urine and faeces. 'Help me, help me,' I'm crying. 'Maman, Papa, help me.'

'No-one is going to help you, Witch. You came here to murder us, but we found you out. Magalie, the pliers.'

My brothers and sisters are hysterical with terror. I hear Eric berating one of them for soiling themselves where they stand. Keisha screams along with me as my brother-in-law twists the pliers, trying to pull the ear off my head.

'Forgive me, forgive me,' I'm whispering. 'Forgive me.'

'Oh no, Witch. I haven't finished with you yet.'

'Then let me die, Eric. I just want to die now.'

'I will not let you die, Witch. I will not allow you to join the devil in Hell. Run the bath, Magalie. Cold.'

I'm being lifted up and the agony redoubles. It feels like every bone in my body is broken. The temperature plummets as we enter the bathroom, and when I'm thrown into the water my skin burns for a moment, then turns icy. I think they've put all of us in the bath, but the others are standing, being hosed down with the shower head. My ears are buzzing, and my eyes refuse to open. I'm so exhausted I couldn't keep my head up if I wanted to.

Keisha's voice in my ear startles me. 'We're going to get you out of this, Kristy. Hang on ...'

A loud crack as someone clubs her. 'Be quiet! No-one speaks to he who has brought kindoki into our home.'

All around me, I can hear splashing, and for a moment I imagine it's summer and we're playing in the fountain.

'She is clean,' says Magalie. 'You, Keisha, out.'

One by one my brothers and sisters are ordered out of the bathroom, until I hear the door close and then Paul's voice on the other side. 'But what about Kris? We need to help Kris.'

'Never mind about the witch; the Devil will take care of him!'

The rest of their words are lost in a riot of crashing and screaming. I'm the big brother. They need me. I try to lift my arm, but I don't have the strength. I try my other arm. Then just my fingers. Nothing.

The bathroom door creaks open. 'The witch needs the next stage of his deliverance,' says Eric. 'Magalie, you know what tools to bring. He still has teeth left in his mouth. The witch will bite us, if we don't smash them out. And his fingers and toes ...'

With the little strength of will I have left, I force my mind to be distracted by happy thoughts, and I remember the gâteau Maman bought at the pâtisserie on Keisha's last birthday. I think of the look of pride on Papa's face when I finished building the wardrobes for my bedroom. When the agony threatens to overwhelm me, I start to list all the boys in my class starting at the back of the room;

Michel, Pierre, Amadou, Gilles. I get as far as the middle of the room before at last, I let myself go.

JESSICA JACKSON

An Overview of Kristy's Case

Kristy Bamu

21.10.95 - 25.12.10

aged 15 years & 2 months

London, England

Kristy lived in Paris with his parents and brothers and sisters. He was doing well at school, and loved playing football. He would train diligently whenever he could, and his sister's boyfriend, Eric Bikubi, had said that he would try to arrange a place for Kristy at an English football academy.

With any other free time he had, Kristy worked on carpentry projects with his father, building his own cupboards and wardrobes for his bedroom. Although Kristy was the second eldest boy of the six children, his older brother's autism meant that the role of 'big brother' fell to Kristy.

Kristy's father, Pierre Bamu, had escaped President Mobutu's dictatorship in the former Zaire (now the Democratic Republic of Congo) and found a home in Paris, where he raised his family, with his wife Jacqueline. A talented man, in his carpentry business, he designs and manufactures furniture for hotels and restaurants. He had hoped his son Kristy would join him in the business one day.

In December 2010, the children made the trip to London, to spend Christmas with their older sister Magalie and her boyfriend Eric. Unable to travel with the children due to business commitments, M. and Mme. Bamu were to join the family for the new year.

Unbeknownst to the Bamu family, Eric Bikubi had a history of making accusations of witchcraft, and had previously forced a female houseguest to cut all the hair from her head, in a bid to rid her of the devil he believed had possessed her. The young woman had managed to escape before much further damage could be done. Although the Bamu family knew that belief in witchcraft (kindoki) existed in the country Pierre Bamu had left many years earlier, they themselves did not believe in it.

At first, all five children were accused of witchcraft. Over a period of three to four days, the children were subjected to various forms of torture under the guise of exorcising their demons; at one point, Bikubi told the children to jump out of the window to see if they could fly. The two girls in particular were beaten repeatedly until Bikubi accepted their confessions that they were witches.

But unfortunately for Kristy, when he got up to use the toilet during the night, he found that the door to the bathroom was locked, and he had the misfortune to wet his pants. And according to some, including Eric Bikubi, this is a sure sign of a witch, and Kristy soon found himself the sole focus of 'deliverance'. Kristy was also accused of causing his older brother's unusual behaviour, when it was, in fact, due to his autism.

And although I have been unable to verify this, a further 'reason' for Eric's persecution of Kristy, is that Bikubi had a son with medical problems, which he blamed on Kristy.

Kristy was struck in the mouth with a hammer, knocking out his teeth. Heavy ceramic floor tiles and bottles were smashed on his head, and a pair of pliers was used to twist his ear halfway off his head. He was cut with a knife, and beaten with a bar used for lifting weights. He had 130 injuries on his body. The other children, whilst injured and terrified, were forced into joining in the violence against their brother.

On Christmas Day, when Bikubi ordered the children into the bath for 'ritual cleansing', Kristy slipped under the water and died from a combination of beating and drowning. Paramedics on the scene described the devastation of the flat, and the hysterical siblings. The girls in particular were badly injured.

Kristy's father, Pierre Bamu, had considered Eric Bikubi a son, and was incredulous when he spoke to his family on the phone on Christmas Day. During one of the calls, Magalie held a knife to her sister's face so that she would not tell her parents what was actually going on. However, on another occasion, Bikubi said he was going to kill Kristy, and when he put him on the phone, the 15 year old boy's last words to his father were to beg him to come and get him, otherwise 'Eric will kill me'.

Pierre Bamu intended to hire a car and drive to England, on the off-chance that there was some truth in what was being said; in case his children actually were in danger. Tragically, due to the holidays and snow storms, the car hire firms were not open, Eurostar was not running, planes were grounded, and by the time the bewildered father was able to travel, his son was already dead.

§

At the trial, the defence argued that evidence of some damage to Bikubi's brain proved that he was not culpable, but the judge did not accept this as sufficient cause to acquit him. Magalie Bamu claimed that she was forced to participate by her boyfriend, but her siblings knew different. The Bamu children had hoped their older sister would save them, but Magalie did the opposite, encouraging Bikubi to beat Kristy until he also confessed to being a witch. One of Kristy's sisters stated: 'Kristy asked for forgiveness. He asked again and again. Magalie did absolutely nothing. She didn't give a damn. She said we deserved it.'

On 5 March 2012, both defendants were found guilty of murder. Eric Bikubi was sentenced to a minimum of thirty years, and Magalie Bamu to a minimum of twenty five years.

§

Kristy's story is one of many in which accusations of demonic possession have been used as an excuse to torture children. For some people, witchcraft is part of their religious belief system, and an adult who fears they have become possessed by a demon, may wish to ask their Pastor for an exorcism, which usually takes the form of ritual prayers.

However, when it is taken to extremes, an innocent child may be singled out as a witch, for the offence of wetting themselves or biting their nails, or being in the same room when someone faints, and be subjected to sadistic methods to 'drive the demon out'.

Dr Richard Hoskins has spent many years studying witchcraft as practised in some African cultures, and he gave evidence at the trial of Eric Bikubi and Magalie Bamu. He made it very clear that the vast majority of Congolese people do not condone the abuse of children under this guise.

Rest Safely in Peace, Kristy

JESSICA JACKSON

A Child is a Human Being!

Bikubi dehumanised Kristy to the extent of viewing him as a supernatural being, possessed by evil spirits.

And throughout time, countless torturers and murderers have dehumanised the objects of their crimes. Whilst psychopaths and sociopaths may be genetically predisposed to feel little or no emotional empathy for their fellow creatures, many others can be trained to dehumanise others, either overtly in conflict and war, or implicitly, by witnessing heartless behaviour within their family or peer group.

Once a caregiver lashes out, in common with most serial abusers, if they don't quit after the first or second time, the die is cast, and they cease to fully see their target as a human being, as much deserving of kindness and understanding as the next person.

This seems particularly true in the case of very young children, with figures from UNICEF stating that the risk of murder by maltreatment is highest in babies under one year old.

We are familiar with the parent who can't relate to their child whilst it is still in the mother's womb. In the vast majority of cases, this lack of interest dissipates the instant they meet their newly born child, and they become a loving parent. But in some cases, a caregiver is unable to bond in a healthy way with the child, with indifference leading to inappropriate responses, and to violence.

There are numerous examples of perpetrators' inability to empathise with the suffering of their children. Tracey Connelly turned her back, playing games and trawling the internet, whilst Baby Peter was being mercilessly tortured within inches of her computer console.

JESSICA JACKSON

The Punch-Bag

When I come round, someone is holding my hand. It feels big and warm and safe. I lie quietly for a few moments, thinking that as long as I don't open my eyes it won't be real. He strokes my fingers and I can almost feel the sadness through his touch. I can't leave him alone any longer.

'Hi, Gregory.'

'Hi, girl.'

'Did we ...? Is it ...?'

'Gone, sweetheart.'

'Are you sure? I mean, could there be a mistake?'

'Oh, honey.'

'No, I'm serious. I've heard about it, where there'd been twins and only one was lost.'

Greg shakes his head. 'I'm sorry. Oh, baby. Don't cry.'

But I'm not crying. I'm howling. Because my heart is being ripped out. This was our last chance; our dream is over.

Greg seems desperate to move out of our home town, even to leave Trinidad, but I know that running far away isn't going to fill up the hole in our lives. But when he's offered the Head of Science post at one of the city's high schools, we decide to go ahead and make the move to San Fernando. We break the news to my mum and dad over Sunday dinner.

'I'm sorry, Mum. But we need a change, a new start. Too many sad memories here.'

She strokes my hair. 'I know, honey. It's been so hard for you.'

'And for you too, Mum. I let you both down. No grand-babies for you. Not unless Celia changes her mind anyway.'

'No, no you didn't, girl. You didn't let us down. And I'll be sure and let you know when your high-and-mighty sister decides to settle herself down with some nice boy and make you an auntie!'

Mum and Dad gather me up in a great big hug. 'We'll miss you so much. And things will be so different there, honey.'

'It's a beautiful city, though,' says Greg. 'The first thing we'll do is go up San Fernando hill and take a good look at our new city.'

Gregory's right. The view is glorious from up high. I feel so free. I'm sure I'm going to like it here.

Greg loves the challenge of his new job. And, oh boy, what a challenge! The broken-down building's in a poor neighbourhood, but he says the kids are bright and keen, even if science does come way down their list of interests.

Jobs for me are hard to come by; I'm over-qualified for this one, under-qualified for that. I spend most of my days walking by the sea or in Skinner Park, trying not to watch the children. Singing in church keeps me going though, and pretty soon I'm making friends with the other women in the choir.

At the social after church, a young white woman about my age grins at me. 'Hey, new girl.'

I've been attending for a few weeks, but I haven't seen her before. 'New girl, yourself.'

'I'm Jo,' she says, putting out her hand. 'Just got back from six weeks visiting family in England. And oh Lord, am I glad to be back!'

A pair of gorgeous six-year-olds in braids and beads hurtle up and almost knock her over with their hugs. 'Auntie Jo, Auntie Jo!'

I retreat back a couple of steps and pretend to admire a display of flaming red chaconia.

I'm helping to clear away the lemonade cups and empty plates when Jo appears at my side.

'You never told me your name.'

'Oh yeah, sorry. It's Sandy. You have a lot of friends here.' I'd been watching a succession of children, all clamouring to give her a cuddle. She'd swing each of the little ones round as they giggled and hooted with excitement, then she'd produce a sweet treat from her fathomless pocket. She'd rock and kiss the babies and let them suck on her finger, and she'd high five the teenagers who stood on the sidelines pretending not to care that she was back. With her curly blonde hair and plump pink cheeks she scarcely looks more than a child herself.

'Kids, eh?' She wipes her forehead with a blue and white neckerchief.

I give a nervous laugh.

'Thought so,' she says, suddenly looking serious.

'What?'

'You don't mind me saying? I mean, we just met.'

'No, it's fine. Go ahead.'

'Loved kids, wanted kids, no kids.'

My tears spring up from somewhere deep.

She touches my arm. 'I'm sorry, honey. But hey, me too.'

'Oh Jo, I'm sorry.'

'Hurts a lot sometimes, doesn't it? Always somebody getting pregnant, even those that don't want to.

Popping out those little uns like they've got to double the population before Easter!'

I can feel that familiar choking in my throat. 'I-I've got to go, Jo. It was nice meeting you.'

'I hope I didn't say the wrong thing, Sandy.'

'No, you said the right thing, Jo. Catch you later, okay?'

'Okay.'

The following Sunday, I find Jo laying out the plates of biscuits. 'I'm sorry I dashed away last week.'

'Oh hey, Sandy. Not at all. I understood. So how come you didn't join the Mothers' Union yet?'

I burst out laughing before I realise she's not joking. 'Because, duh-uh; I'm not a mother.'

'Didn't let a little thing like that stop me.'

'Really? Back home, you had to be a mother, you know, to qualify.'

She shakes her head, then laughs. 'Well here in San Fernando they'll take anybody.' She nudges me. 'Even you!'

She meets me at the door on Tuesday at seven. 'You nervous?'

'A bit.'

'You needn't be. They're not a bad crowd.'

A stout middle-aged woman in a loud flowery dress, complete with a pink hat and pearls strides past.

Jo rolls her eyes. 'Elvira. Her heart's in the right place, even if I don't know whether to sit on her or draw her across the window.'

I snigger like a big kid.

Jo was right though. They're a good crowd, and the variety of things we discuss is mind-boggling. Jo elbows me when we get on to the subject of the Children's Home.

'Can anyone think of anywhere to find more volunteers?' says Marcia, a striking woman with a fabulous afro. 'We're all working flat out and we really need people to spend time with the children one-to-one.'

'Sandy here would like to join us,' says Jo, as I choke on my lemonade. 'She's really great with the littlest ones. The newborns.'

'That's fantastic,' says Marcia. 'Can you get there tomorrow afternoon, say about two?'

'But I don't know …'

'She'll be there,' says Jo.

For the first few minutes all I want to do is hand him back and run. I'm so tense I'm sure I must be doing him more harm than good. Then Jo nods and moves off to the far end of the nursery, and there's just me and Leo.

At least he's not crying, so that's a start. I look around, then raise my arms higher, put my nose to his head and breathe. Oh, that beautiful smell. Ever so gently, I rest my cheek against his, and the softness brings a lump to my throat. 'Mmm, you gorgeous, lovely boy.' I hold him away again so I can see his round brown eyes and shock of bushy hair. 'Aren't you, Leo? Aren't you the most gorgeous boy in the world?' And for the first time, the smile doesn't need to be coaxed onto my lips. Leo shows me his gums and gurgles. I chuckle back at him and his eyes shine as he makes a grab for my finger.

'Hi there, Mum,' say Jo as she walks past, a toddler on each hip.

'Most of them go back, Sandy.'

'To their parents?'

'Yeah, they're often no more than kids themselves. And they just need a break from all that responsibility.'

I nod.

'Think you can do it, Sandy?'

'Do what?'

'Love 'em while they're here, and then let 'em go?'

'I don't know. I think so.'

'First time's the worst. You think you'll never get over your broken heart.' She shrugs. 'But you do.'

By the time autumn comes I'm spending every day at the Home. Gregory comes with me most Saturdays, and sometimes I see him watching me, a wistful look on his face.

'You happy, hun?'

'Yeah, very.'

He comes up behind me and wraps his arms around me, clasping his hands against my tummy. 'Love you, Sandy.'

Amy arrives on a blustery day when the Home is already overflowing. Elvira practically dumps the little girl in my arms. 'One-to-one, Sandy. Won't be ready to mingle for a while yet. Get Jo to help you when she needs the toilet.'

'But I can manage, Elvira.'

'Trouble down below. Let Jo help you.'

'But, what ...'

She gives me a long look.

'Oh, I see.'

'You probably don't. Worst I've ever seen.' Then she softens a little. 'The stepfather. Don't worry, Jo knows what to do.'

The child looks terrified, and that first day I just sit her beside me while I rock and sing to baby Theodore. But I ache to hold her in my arms, stroke my fingers lightly across her burns and bruises, and make them disappear.

Amy can't bear to be touched by anyone. Any voice above a whisper makes her tremble. She's just shy of her third birthday, her serious little face permanently knit into an anxious frown, her shoulder length hair matted into dry, almost grey locks. And when Greg arrives that Saturday she scrambles off her perch beside me and makes for the door, leaving a wet patch on the seat.

I fall in love with her instantly. Only new mothers seeing their baby for the first time will know what I mean. Sorry Greg, I love you and all that, but I wouldn't walk through fire for you.

I search for Amy the moment I come on shift, and I fuss and tarry when it's time for me to leave. When a colleague takes her away for a bath, or a sleep, or a snack, it takes all my strength not to snatch her back and squeeze her into my breast.

One Thursday, I'm an hour late, and as soon as I enter the play-room my eyes find hers, anxiously searching, and her face lights up into the first beautiful smile she has ever given me. I rush over and scoop her up into my arms. All that day, she clings to me, crying if anyone tries to prise her hands from around my neck. I kiss her hair, her cheeks, any part of her I can reach, and I pretend I'm doing it all for her sake.

'Loving detachment, Sandy,' says Elvira as she tickles Amy under the chin. 'Loving detachment.'

I nod, but I can't help myself. I hide round corners with her in my arms, so that I can cuddle her closer and whisper that I love her.

Jo arrives in the afternoon and I see her glance over at me as Marcia is giving her the morning's update. Frank as ever, Jo comes right up to me. 'Let me have her.'

'Please Jo, no. Look at her; look how happy she is.'

'I'm looking at *you*, Sandy. How you need this, how you need her to love you.' She shakes her head. 'I know the pain of loss, Sandy, and the gaping hole it leaves behind.'

'Just today then, Jo. Let me be her mum just for today.'

My friend smiles in spite of her effort to be strict with me. 'I'll check with Marcia.'

After a quick chat on the other side of the room, Jo nods over at me.

The rest of that day are the happiest few hours of my life. Now at last I know how it feels to have a little person depend on me, and to have the joy of meeting her every need.

Okay, yes I confess, I do pretend that she's my child. I brush the remaining tangles out of her hair and am surprised to see how much it looks like mine, straighter and glossier now, with a little curl all along the bottom. I hold her up to the mirror, cheek to cheek with me, and we both smile at our reflection. We clap our hands, I show her some colours, we count up to ten. I watch over her as she takes her nap and I stroke her cheek.

I whisper that Mummy loves her and that she's safe now, and I am going to take care of her. I am selfish to the bone.

Jo comes up behind me and puts her hand on my shoulder. 'Just for today, Sandy.'

'Alright, alright I know.' I've never snapped at Jo before and am immediately sorry. 'I do know. She's someone else's little girl, and she'll probably go back.'

Jo squeezes my shoulder.

'But she's just so gorgeous,' I say. 'I'll be good though, I promise.'

And after that day, I *am* good. On the outside.

I share Amy's care with the other volunteers; I don't tell her I love her (at least not too often), I don't promise her the moon.

'My Lord,' says Elvira, as she watches Amy playing with the huge doll's house. 'That baby's coming along so fast!'

'She's amazing, isn't she?'

Amy knows we're talking about her, and toddles over to us. 'Hi Sandy. Hi Vira.'

'What game is that, Amy?' asks Elvira.

'Good mummies and daddies,' she says. 'Like Sandy and Geg. No smacking. No hurting.'

'My, how she can talk now!' Elvira shakes her head. 'You need to be proud of yourself, Sandy.'

Amy giggles. 'Proud, Sandy.'

'Where've you been hiding that precious smile? You're such a pretty girl, aren't you, Amy?'

She points at her chest. 'Pretty girl.' Then she looks up shyly. 'Cuddle for Amy?'

Elvira laughs and crouches down beside her. 'Of course, honey.'

Amy grabs my sleeve. 'Cuddle for Amy?'

'I've always got cuddles for you, sweetheart.'

'And doesn't she know it!' laughs Elvira.

'More cuddles for Amy?' she says reaching up to me again.

A few weeks later, Jo bounds up to me as I walk through the door. 'It's happened,' she says, hugging me. 'She's not going back.'

I know who she means. 'You're sure?'

She nods. 'Come and help me with the paperwork.'

I try to help her, but all I can do is point to the second item on the form. 'Jo, Amy was born on the day of my last still-birth. That's part of why I love her so much. I'm sure of it.'

'Oh, Sandy.'

'There's a bond between us, you know there is. I've always felt it.' I'm crying now. 'Please let me go and be with her, Jo.'

'Okay, honey.' She smiles. 'The things people do to get out of doing paperwork!'

But I'm already dashing off to the playroom.

Over the next few weeks, Amy begins to smile more, even laugh a little. She joins in a few of the jumping games, and occasionally plays in the sandpit with the other toddlers. She even smiles at the sight of Greg's big grin, though she remains terrified of all other men.

Gregory and me are top of the list for adopting Amy. We can't wait to be her real parents and be a proper family.

We decorate her bedroom in her favourite colours, and buy pretty dresses for church, and denim dungarees to play in. We can't help ourselves. I start staying overnight at the Children's Home, so that I can become accustomed to Amy's sleep pattern and be there if she needs anything.

She adores Greg now. When I see her look up at him as he takes her tiny hand in his big paw, my heart swells. Then we take her into the garden and swing her along between us and she giggles and shouts, 'More,' at the top of her voice. She loves the little slide; as long as one of us is there to catch her and give her an extra cuddle for being a brave girl.

One morning, Jo greets me at the door, her usually ruddy cheeks as white as cotton. 'Come and sit in the garden, Sandy.'

'You okay, Jo?'

'Yeah. Yeah, I'm fine.' She pats the place on the bench beside her. 'Sandy, oh Sandy, I'm sorry. Amy's grandmother has asked for custody.'

'No, oh no. But she can't, they can't … I thought they said she'd never be returned to her family.'

'Not to her mother and the stepfather who abused her, no. But this is different. With the grandmother, there's no record of abuse. And she's family, Sandy.'

'We're her family now. We love her.'

'I know you do.'

'He'll get to her, Jo. He'll do all those terrible things to her again.'

'Shush now, Sandy.'

I hadn't even noticed I was wailing.

'He's not allowed to see her. At least not on his own. The grandmother is a good woman.'

'I hope she is, Jo.'

She looks at her watch. 'It's morning story-time. But you wait here a while.'

I grab her hand. 'Will she get her, Jo?'

My friend nods. 'I think so, honey.'

When the decision is confirmed, I try very hard to begin distancing myself from Amy, for her sake. I don't really succeed. On the day she has to leave, I go to the Home and hold her for the last time.

Jo and Elvira have explained to her that she is going to live with Granny now and she will be able to see her mummy again.

She looks confused. 'Mummy?' she says to me.

'Say good-bye to her, Sandy,' whispers Jo.

I know I risk upsetting Amy further, but I clutch her to my breast, until they have to drag me away from her.

Jo takes my hand and guides me to a place at the window where I watch the social worker strap her into her seat and hand her the cuddly bunny we gave her on her birthday. I see Amy smile at the woman, then twist her head, searching.

Jo squeezes my hand as the tears fall. 'It's okay, honey. Let it go.'

I run outside and watch the car roll up the street and out of sight.

For the rest of the day, I trudge around the city. Everything seems wrong. The buildings appear to lean over as if ready to topple upon the cars and people below. A newspaper seller barks in my ear, urging passers-by to buy the Trinidad Express. I watch in horror as his features seem to melt and his nose elongates and reaches his chin. I look away, and crash into a woman whose eyes bore into me as she spits, 'Mind where you're going.' I almost collide with a cyclist as I run to the beach, where I take off my shoes and stumble along the rocks and sand.

Greg finds me later that day, in a secluded corner of Skinner Park, rocking back and forth, my arms clasped round my knees. I don't remember how I got there.

He half-carries me home. 'Do you want the doctor, honey?'

'No, I want Amy. I want my baby girl.'

Every day, Gregory makes me sandwiches before he sets off to work, and every day I hide them at the bottom of the bin. If he didn't insist on bathing me and cleaning my teeth, I wouldn't get out of bed.

I say my prayers every night for Amy, hoping the grandmother is protecting her and loving her. Surely she must be. Who could hurt that baby? Then I remember that before she came to the Mothers' Union Home, Amy was dumped at the hospital and no-one came to visit her. No-one came to claim her. Surely that wouldn't happen again? Who could not love her? But. If it did happen, if they were caught yelling at her or abandoning her somewhere, then maybe they'd take her away again and let me have her. Then I'd have the chance to show Amy what it's like to be truly loved. She'd be my baby. My daughter. My prayers take a different turn.

I've started going for walks again. Between my prayers I talk to Amy. I tell her I'll be coming for her soon. I let the sea breeze blow my words across the beach, sending them to her, so she knows I still love her. I've started going back to church. I've even dropped in at the children's home once or twice, praying she'll be back. Maybe next time, I tell myself.

One day, Greg comes home from work, more ashen and drawn than I've ever seen him. He won't even look at me.

'What is it, honey? Is it school? Has something happened?'

He's trembling; he can't speak.

'We can sort it out, Greg. Whatever it is.'

'Jo rang me.'

Before I can figure out what he's trying to say, there's a knock on the door; who can be disturbing us when I need to comfort my husband? Jo walks straight in. Her face is covered in fiery blotches and her eyes are so puffy I can hardly tell if they're open or closed.

I look from her to Greg; neither of them will meet my eye, and I whisper, 'Amy?'

Jo makes me sit down, and Greg takes my hand. A glass of rum appears from nowhere.

'The stepfather?'

They both just look at me, unwilling to trample on my heart.

I can't stop screaming. After two hours, they call the doctor and I am sedated and admitted to St Ann's.

I've been here two months now. They say my health is slowly improving; at least I don't scream and cry 24/7 anymore. I join in the craft sessions and paint Amy's picture over and over again. One morning I draw the doorframe he hung her from, and the nurse says that although it's good to let my feelings out I should perhaps stop punching the canvas now that it lay in splinters at my feet.

Jo visits often. She tells me there are too many children at the Home for them to cope with. If only they had another pair of hands. But when Marcia comes one day and I mention how busy they are she looks puzzled and says they've never been so quiet.

Mum and Dad stay for the first couple of weeks; making hearty meals for Greg and bringing in a plate every day for me. When I leave the hospital, in a few more weeks, they're coming back to San Fernando to take care of me. To them, I'll always be their precious baby girl.

Just as Amy, in my heart, will always be mine.

JESSICA JACKSON

An Overview of Amy's Case

Amy Emily Annamunthodo

07.05.02 - 15.05.06

aged 4 years

Marabella, San Fernando

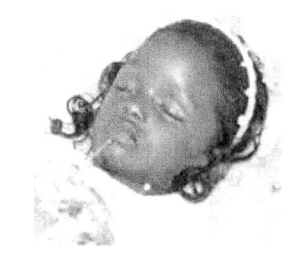

Trinidad

I can find no photos of Emily when she was alive

Amy, who was often called Emily by her family, was born in Trinidad to Anita Annamunthodo and Jason Walker. The couple separated when Amy was still a young baby, and Walker was not involved in his daughter's life. From the time of Amy's birth, Anita's mother, Chanardai Basedo, regularly cared for her baby granddaughter.

After Anita took up with Marlon King, a security guard twenty years her senior, with three older children of his own, Amy was admitted to San Fernando hospital a number of times with fractures and bruising. In May 2005, at the age of three, Amy was yet again taken to hospital, but this time she was abandoned there. There were plans to make her a ward of the state, and she was placed in the Mothers' Union Children's Home in San Fernando. Amy had delayed speech and poor general development but she began to thrive in this loving environment.

However, tragically for Amy, it was deemed safe for her to be returned to the custody of her grandmother in December 2005. When Mrs Basedo became ill, Amy's 'care' was taken over by her mother and stepfather, and her fate was sealed. Within four months of leaving the sanctuary of the children's home, Amy was dead. The little girl had been starved, beaten, burned with cigarettes on her vagina and thighs, and she had been raped and sodomised. She was regularly locked in a room with a cloth stuffed in her mouth to muffle her cries.

§

Marlon King was notorious in his neighbourhood for his violent behaviour. He had once body-slammed a woman onto a cart, thrown grass upon her, and threatened to set her alight. On another occasion he had stripped a woman naked and dragged her through the streets. Neighbours were so afraid of him that they did not dare to challenge him, despite witnessing his brutality to his stepdaughter. We can only imagine the horror of Amy's life with a man who appears to have repeatedly terrorised women and children.

During the five month trial, it was stated that on the day her daughter died, Amy's mother was out of the house, and a neighbour, Andre Rocke had been visiting King. As Rocke was leaving, he said he felt the wooden house shaking, and returned to peer through a crack in the woodwork. Rocke testified that he had witnessed Marlon King hanging Amy up by her hair attached to a door frame, and punching her twenty to thirty times. The child was gagged with a plastic bag in her mouth. It seems that Rocke did not intervene to stop the beating, nor alert the emergency services.

The pathologist testified that Amy's liver, spleen, kidneys and heart were ruptured as she swung from the door frame, while King yelled, 'Hush your mouth'. The massive haemorrhaging caused by the beating caused her death after about fifteen minutes. At his trial, King denied beating Amy, alleging instead that her mother, Anita, was the one who had done so. And furthermore, he then also claimed that it was Rocke who was guilty of inflicting Amy's injuries upon her. Perhaps we will never know the truth. What we do know, is that Rocke did not seek help for Amy.

Marlon King's version of events was that on that day, he had gone into Amy's room to find her 'humming and crying'. She then soiled herself and King insisted that she clean herself up. When Anita Annamunthodo returned home, King went out to visit a neighbour, only to be summoned back by Anita, as Amy was 'stretched out' and still. That evening, the pair took Amy to the Accident and Emergency Department, although Amy was already dead, and rigor mortis had begun to set in.

The summing up of the case took five days. Before they left to consider their verdict, Justice Anthony Carmona offered jurors an alternative to finding King guilty of murder. If they felt that the accused was provoked into killing Amy, because on that day he was suffering from a toothache, and her defecating in her underwear and her crying had pushed him too far(!), they could return a verdict of manslaughter. The jury took only two hours to consider the evidence, and just before they delivered their verdict, King interrupted the forewoman, saying that he wanted to explain himself. But the verdict, that he was guilty of Amy's murder, was immediately given, before he had chance to speak much further.

§

Amy's mother, Anita Annamunthodo, served 11 months in jail for neglect, and for Amy's murder, her stepfather, Marlon King, was sentenced in March 2012 to death by hanging. While other members of the family were not always able to attend the trial, Amy's maternal grandfather, Hajji Annamunthodo, was present in court every day, and broke the news of the death sentence to his wife Chanardai.

§

A year after Amy's murder, whilst King was in custody before his trial, screams were heard coming from his cell, where he was being beaten by a group of fellow inmates. Police Prosecutor, Sergeant Harricharan Kassy, reported that King had been used as a punch-bag by several other prisoners who had kicked, punched and tried to strangle him. King was taken to the same hospital that Amy had been admitted to several times to be treated for her injuries and neglect at the hands of her mother and King. The outcome of King's experience as a human punch-bag did not match that of his little victim. King, who suffered a number of small injuries, including bruising around the eyes, was treated and released after about an hour.

In January 2021, King's attorney, Peter Carter, lodged an appeal against his conviction, citing in particular the unfair use of hearsay evidence. He called into question the testimony of King's ex-wife, who had reportedly been beaten multiple times before she escaped her husband, and the evidence of Andre Rocke, who King claims is the actual murderer of Amy. Carter also accused the trial judge, Anthony Carmona, of "usurping the function of the jury in his directions on the issue of credibility" and said "his review of the weaknesses of the State's case was deficient". The outcome of the appeal is yet to be announced.

> **My thanks to Althea from Trinidad for her insights into Amy's story.**
>
> **Rest Safely in Peace, Amy**

JESSICA JACKSON

Returning Children to their Abuser

Despite Amy beginning to thrive in the Mother's Union home, she was returned to her family, to be viciously tortured to death.

There must be many cases when authorities make the correct decision to allow a child to be returned to their caregiver. For example, if the situation that brought about the abuse has been resolved; the parents are over their 'bad patch', are clean of drugs and alcohol, free of an abusive partner, have gained a strong support network, and have learnt to become mature and loving parents.

Too often, however, children are sent back home to their doom. In the next story, you will read that a judge agreed not to return the two boys to their cruelly abusive mother, and yet made a different decision for their little sister.

It is hard to see the sense behind a decision to return a child who expresses fear of their caregiver, either verbally or nonverbally (which even young babies can demonstrate), to a life of torture.

Hiding the Torture

Some caregivers hide their children from prying eyes, as we will see in the next story. Others become proficient in hiding the scars and bruises in front of others. Babies' faces are smothered in cream or chocolate, hats and long-sleeved clothing cover burns and bruises, and the child is yet again 'asleep' or 'not at home' when the social worker visits.

Agencies are told that the child has a particular illness that is causing them to lose weight, that the burns on their skin were self-inflicted when the child pulled a pan of hot water over itself, that the bruises appeared when they were fighting with their siblings, or that a piece of furniture fell on them, causing their bones to break; the list goes on.

But others hide the child away completely, limiting visits by family members, and withdrawing the victim from school.

The Bit in the Middle

Now that we're halfway through the book, I'd like to share my ideas on prevention and the warning signs to look out for. Perhaps you have ideas of your own?

Can We Prevent These Murders?

There are no easy solutions, but these are my own views, which I cover in the pages of my books, echoing the advice of the World Health Organisation (WHO).

1 – End physical discipline of children
2 – Regulate homeschooling effectively
3 – An outlet for caregivers' anger
4 – Listen to the children when they report abuse
5 – Improve communication between agencies
6 – Safe places for unwanted babies
7 – Educate the parents of the future:
- that a baby communicates by crying
- how to give love, safety and guidance
- about bladder & bowel habits of children

In an ideal world, children would not be brought into an environment where drugs and/or violence abound, or where they are unwanted, or are wanted only to meet the impossible-to-meet needs of a parent. But to protect the ones who are already born, we need adequate support, education and a joined-up system where an abused child does not fall through the cracks.

Warning Signs of Abuse

There are various factors that might suggest a child is being abused. This list has been compiled by the NSPCC, but is by no means exhaustive:

- unexplained changes in behaviour or personality
- becoming withdrawn or anxious
- becoming uncharacteristically aggressive
- lacking social skills and having few friends
- poor bonding or relationship with a parent
- knowledge of adult issues inappropriate for their age
- running away or going missing
- wearing clothes which cover their body

And I would add:

- marks and bruises on the body
- being secretive
- stealing (often food)
- weight loss
- inappropriate clothing
- poor hygiene / unkempt appearance
- tiredness
- inability to concentrate
- being overly eager to please the adult
- the child telling you that they're being hurt

- a non-verbal child showing you that they're being hurt
- the adult removing the child from school after they have come under suspicion

If you suspect an adult of abusing a child, don't unquestioningly accept what they say, but instead:

        A – Assume nothing

        B – Be vigilant

        C – Check everything

        D – Do something

Listen to the children and report what you see:

TO REPORT CHILD ABUSE IN THE USA & CANADA
The National Child Abuse Hotline: 1-800-422-4453
If a child is in immediate danger, call 911

TO REPORT CHILD ABUSE IN THE UK
For adults, call the NSPCC on 0808 800 5000
For children, call Childline on 0800 1111
Or if there is risk of imminent danger, ring 999

TO REPORT CHILD ABUSE IN AUSTRALIA
The National Child Abuse Reportline: 131-478
Children, call: 1800-55-1800
If a child is in immediate danger, call 000

Ready to carry on?

Homeschool

'Keep them up, girl. What's wrong with you? Keep them up like I tell you.'

But my arms are aching so much; I can't keep them up for another second.

'So, I guess you want this, then? Huh, you want this?'

The belt is never far from her side. Each day a little stiffer with my blood.

When I start to scream she whacks me in the mouth with her shoe before leaving the room. Will she let me alone now? But I know she's only gone for a moment, and I hear the click of the plug into the socket, and the hum of the vacuum cleaner starting up.

'Scream all you want now, girl. Nobody gonna hear you. And nobody gonna care.'

After a few minutes she turns the belt around and uses the buckle end. That's what hurts the most; the metal cutting my face.

She shakes her head. 'Fifteen years old and squealing like a new born.'

When she's exhausted, she nods towards my piece of cardboard, meaning it's over for now and I can lie down, making sure to keep my blood off the carpet. Then she trudges out of the room, the vacuum cleaner goes quiet, and my little half-brother is asking what's for dinner.

The next day she sits at the window in silence. Waiting for me to move. My arms feel like they're being torn from their sockets, and my legs are shaking.

'Close your eyes, bitch.'

I hear her rustle her magazine. Clear her throat. Turn the page. Settle down again. I try not to breathe too loudly. When her gentle snoring begins, I do my exercises. Stretch the toes; left foot, right foot. Now my fingers and wrists. I risk opening an eye. She's definitely napping. I allow my arms to fall; I've perfected the art of raising them in a flash if she suddenly wakes up. I peer through half-open eyelids and watch the dust motes dancing in the thin beam of sunlight shining in through a gap in the curtains. They're pretty.

Her snoring goes on, and I swing my arms round like a windmill, hoping she won't sense the movement of the air between us. But there's something tickling my throat, and I'm sure I'm going to cough. I swallow hard, tense my throat muscles, and try to press my fingers into the hollow at the front of my neck. That sometimes works. I mustn't cough; mustn't make a sound.

My right hand's no good anymore, but I'm pressing with my left index finger and the urge to cough is fading. If only Mom would let me have a drink of water when

I'm thirsty, maybe my throat wouldn't be so dry. A few tears seep through my eyelids and I try to choke back my sobs. But she stirs.

'Can't a busy mother grab a few winks of sleep without you disturbing my quiet time?'

I tense and wait for the lash of the belt.

'Chrissakes, just lie down and be quiet.' She folds her arms across her belly and leans back again.

Maybe I'll try to sleep too.

When I wake up, I can tell she's not in the room anymore. I hear children's voices. Most afternoons after school they run helter-skelter up and down the stairs, then one of them will sneak in here and pass me a biscuit or a piece of bread. I have to try and hide it, or wolf it down, or they'll be in for it. Or maybe my stepfather's mom, Grandma Lynn, will have managed to get past Mom, and she's handing out Herschey bars, and Patti will try and bring me a bite later.

I've set myself the task of making up some more stories to help me drift away from the pain when she next comes for me. I try not to use them up when I'm just here on my own. I've got one where Mom and Randy and Patti and me go to the park and Randy falls over and I cuddle him better. I haven't cuddled my half-brother or sister in a long time.

There's another story that I keep for the worst times. In that one, Mom comes to Cascade Middle School to meet me, and the teacher tells Mom about the poem I wrote about how much I love her. And Mom looks pleased and tells the teacher, 'Yes, I love her too. She's a good girl. I'm so proud of her.' She takes me to the diner and my school-friends wave at me through the window and see that I've got a proper mom after all. Mom lets me eat a cheeseburger and ice-cream with maple syrup. Even Randy and Patti aren't in that one; it's just me and Mom. And food.

Then there's the one where God comes down and saves me, but I don't tell myself that one too often anymore. It just makes me sad when he doesn't come.

My tummy growls.

'Shut up, you piece of shit.' She must've snuck back in here while I was day-dreaming. She's pulled her chair up close so she can kick me. 'I'm gonna get you later, you little runt. I've got some new things to try.' She's so close I can smell her breath.

My bowels churn and release.

'What the hell? You dirty bitch. Just you damn well wait.'

She goes out and slams the door. A second's relief before the fear kicks back in. If only it was just the same things every time. I could float away, watch from above as she does it to that rag doll of a girl down there. But she's always experimenting. She calls it 'play-time'. The toys are a bit different to the toys I've seen other kids play with. I pray she doesn't come back with the red stick.

Patti is crying.

I can hear Mom yelling. 'Get out into that yard. Now!'

I'm sick into my mouth. The neighbourhood dogs mooch around a piece of ground out back. Their owners don't pick up.

'Out. Right. Now.'

The door slams. A few minutes later I hear Mom screaming. 'That's not enough! Chrissakes, Patti. Can't you do it right? Don't end up like your dumb-ass sister.'

The door slams again. A couple of the dogs bark half-heartedly at her. I know Patti's scared of them and I wish I could be there to protect her like a big sister should. Like I used to.

I hear Mom again. 'That's better. And it's nice and fresh. Good girl. Go on up and leave it by the closet.'

My sister places the familiar blue plastic bowl on the floor. 'I'm sorry, Jeanette.'

I gag and try to form the words the best way I can. 'I know. It's okay.'

It's not too long before Mom comes up the stairs. I used to beg her not to do it, but it only encouraged her. I pray a little, not too much though. Doesn't make a speck of difference.

She pads across the room in her pink slippers. 'Look what those nice doggies gone and done for you today, girl.'

The sun is moving round, edging behind the gates of the lumber yard. I think she's finished for the day. I hear the front door shut as she goes out to the bar. She did bring the stick. It's just a twig or a branch from outside, but she's made it pointed somehow and the red colour is blood. The flesh on my thigh's been whipped so hard it's rotted down to the bone, and Mom pretends she's being kind when she scrapes out the stinking wound. But I know she finds it funny to jab my bone with the stick and watch me writhe. I couldn't think of any stories, and instead I remembered the time I was left alone in the den, and I got out of the house and started to run. But my legs were weak and I couldn't see properly and I fell onto the sidewalk. A neighbour brought me back, though I begged her not to . I sometimes imagine her being made to eat hot, steaming dog shit.

Another day. I'm not sure where she is. Oh wait, there's a faint smell of fries; I guess they're finishing up supper.

When she comes up, she'll turn on the vacuum cleaner again and leave it halfway up the stairs. She likes me to scream, but she doesn't want the little ones to hear everything. She hides some of it from Richard, my stepfather, too. It's harder for her since he had his heart attack and can't go out to work though. I think he knows what Mom does but he doesn't say a lot. I wish he would stand up to Mom sometimes and tell her not to hurt me.

Sometimes, at night, she puts me out in the yard. It's padlocked, of course, but the light comes on as I move around, brushing up. It's not too bad, because if it rains, I can drop down to a puddle and lap like a cat. The snow's good too, because I can put out my tongue and feel its freshness.

I often think of my two big brothers when I'm out in the yard. I wish I could see them again. We had a lot of fun back when I lived with them and our foster mom and dad in California. I once had a birthday party with a Winnie the Pooh cake. And I got a Pooh backpack for school. My brothers teased the heck out of me, but I think they secretly liked him too. We used to laugh a lot. Our foster dad called us the Giggle Team, and we'd laugh even more.

After our real mom got out of jail, my brothers didn't come back to live with us. And they stayed in California when Mom and me moved to Oregon. That's a long way away. I miss them so much and I get sad again, thinking about how different it all is now.

That's when I wonder if there's any other kids out there; in yards all over the country, all over the world maybe, cold and starving and dreading the morning.

Mom and me are downstairs in the kitchen when I hear people talking through the open window and I freeze, recognising the voices. Someone knocks quietly; Mom doesn't seem to have heard it, because she belts me again. They knock again, louder.

'What the hell?' says Mom. 'Why are folks always coming round here trying to make trouble?'

Thank goodness, she's not going to answer it. 'Yeah, Mom. We don't need visitors, do we?'

She looks at me sideways, and it becomes another game. 'Well, I'm not sure about that. It could be somebody important. Maybe even some little friends of yours.'

I can hear Billy's voice. 'I'm sure they're home. Try again, Amanda.'

Mom looks as if she can't wait to open the door now. 'Well now, if it isn't your school-friends come calling.'

'Mom, don't let them in. Please, don't let them in.'

'Don't be rude, Jeanette. Don't you think it's nice of your friends to come visit with you?'

As she turns the handle, I edge further into the corner and stand as still as a statue.

'Well, hello there!'

'Hello, Mrs McAnulty,' says Amanda. 'We've come to see Jeanette.'

'Isn't that nice? But should I let you in or not? It sure don't seem polite leaving you standing out there on the doorstep.'

'We won't stay long, Mrs McAnulty,' says Billy.

'The hell you won't,' says Mom, under her breath. She sighs. 'Sorry, folks. I can't do it. What she's got could be catching.'

'Is Jeanette coming back to school, Mrs McAnulty?'

'No, she isn't, Amanda.'

'Is she okay?'

'She's fine,' says Mom.

'Jeanette. Jeanette,' whispers Billy. 'Come to the door. We can't see you.'

'That's enough now,' says Mom. 'She gets tired easy.'

'Will you give her this please, Mrs McAnulty?' Billy hands Mom a Snickers.

'That's kind.' She beams at my friends, then turns to me. 'Honey, why don't you go upstairs and lie down? I'll be up to see to you in a few minutes.'

She takes a bite of the Snickers bar between every beat of her fist into my face.

When I was still going to school, Amanda and me were best friends. Tommy-Lee liked her, and Billy liked me. We liked them back, too. Billy once passed me a note in class, and he got in big trouble, but he said later it was worth it and then he tried to kiss me. I didn't let him, but I wanted to. He said I was the prettiest girl in school. One day when the four of us were sitting together in the cafeteria, Amanda noticed that my lunch-box only had one cracker and a small piece of cheese in it. She showed me her tuna sandwiches and Twinkies and I started to cry. She sent the boys away, and put her arm round me and gave me a Twinkie. She asked if Mom was hurting me, and a bit later I saw her talking to Miss Mullins, the nice lady who works in the cafeteria. Miss Mullins started giving me snacks after that.

Then two ladies from the Department of Human Services came to the house. They glanced at me and then I was sent out of the room. I could hear them through the wall.

'She's impossible,' Mom told them. 'The lies she tells.'

'It must be hard on you. And she's very thin. Does she have an eating disorder?'

'An eating disorder? Oh yes, yes that's right. We try our best, but you know what they're like.'

'Well, if you need any more support …'

'Oh, thank you. But we're fine.'

The ladies never came back. I sometimes imagine the short one being forced to stand still for hours with her arms up in the air. Or the tall one with glasses being beaten in the mouth with a shoe.

After that, Mom took me out of school; she told everybody I was going to be homeschooled.

One time, when Richard's mom came to see us, another lady came with her. She was the most beautiful person I'd ever seen.

'I'm your step-dad's cousin, Mary,' she said. 'And I've got kids your age. Next time, I'll bring them with me and we'll all go to the play-park.'

We tried not to look too excited; we knew Mom wouldn't like it. We didn't think it would ever happen, but a couple of weeks later, they all came over. Grandma Lynn stayed home and helped Mom clean house, and we had an amazing time at the park. Mary's kids were full of fun, and I guess they found us a bit quiet at first, but soon

Randy was racing around, squealing and laughing with the other little ones.

Mary had made a picnic, and we all tucked into jelly sandwiches and Oreos. And Pepsi. Patti and me tried our best to be polite, but it was hard not to cram all that lovely food into our mouths as quickly as we could.

'Hey, Jeanette,' said Mary as I helped her to clear up. 'Is everything okay at home, hon?'

I turned redder than a stop light. 'Oh yeah, yeah it's great.'

'If ever things aren't okay ....'

'Things are fine.'

Mary must've said something to Mom though, because after they'd gone, we all got a beating and we didn't get to see Mary again.

Mom's brought me down to the kitchen, taken off her shoe and is crashing it across my face. My lips feel like they're being torn from my mouth. Patti and Randy are pretending to play quietly in the corner. My little sister's eyes glisten as she mouths the words, 'I love you', whenever Mom's back is turned.

Mom stops, arm in mid-air, at a knock on the door.

'Who the hell?' she mutters, and motions for me to be quiet, and stand facing the wall with my arms above my head. I try and try but it's still so hard to do that. Even after a few seconds you can feel your muscles burning.

The knocking starts again. Louder.

'Jesus Christ!' Mom flings open the door.

My stepfather's mom stands red-faced on the doorstep.

Mom bars her way. 'I *told* you you're not welcome here anymore!'

'Let me see the kids, Angela. Please. I won't stay long.'

Mom moves aside. 'Just a few minutes, Lynn. I mean it.'

'Hey, kids,' says Grandma, as Patti and Randy rush up to her. She grabs one under each arm and squeezes before turning my way. 'What the hell's going on with Jeanette? No wonder you didn't want me to see her!'

'She's being punished, is all. You know what a bad girl she is.'

Mom had warned us all to tell Grandma I was alright. So we try to. But my words whistle uselessly past my flapping lips, making no sense at all. Even trying to smile probably results in an ugly grimace.

'Angela, listen to me.'

'You got something to say, just say it.'

'We can take the kids. Mary would love to have Jeanette; you know that.'

'You think I can't take care of my own kids? Huh? Is that what you're saying?' Mom has gotten up close to Grandma, pointing her finger right in her face.

'We'd take real good care of them. You know we would.'

'Get out of my house, you nosy bitch.'

Grandma takes hold of me, and I want to go with her so bad, but Mom is stronger. Grandma yells that she's going to Family Services again and this time she'll make them listen. Mom tells her she'd better take a good look at us kids then, because it'd be the last time she'd see us.

I know I've changed. I caught my reflection in the bathroom mirror one time, and I don't think Billy would say I was pretty now. Everyone used to say I looked like Mom. Dark hair, dark eyes. Mexican blood from way back. Or is it Native American? But now? Not for those of a nervous disposition. R-rated. Like the horror movies my stepdad likes to watch.

Mom had said that if I could stop talking nonsense and shivering "for five godamn minutes" I could have a slice of turkey at Thanksgiving. But I didn't manage it. Maybe at Christmas. My head hurts so much, and I can't remember if it's me or Mom who's been bashing it against the floor. I seem to recall her holding up another red-stained tree branch and showing my little sister some sort of hole on the back of my head. 'If you stab someone there,' she told Patti, who was beginning to cry. 'It would give them brain damage.'

The blood that's been pouring from my wounds is hardening on my face and neck. My head feels funny and I don't know whether it's day or night. And I just want to sleep. Most of the time Mom lets me lie on my piece of cardboard, and though it's sodden it feels so comfortable that I sleep for hours. I can't even feel the hunger pangs that used to keep me awake. Also, God has spoken to me. At last. He says from now on he's definitely not going to ignore me and he's going to look after me and everything's going to be alright.

There's a lot of noise, but it seems to be in the distance. My stepfather's yelling orders at Mom. 'Put her in a cold bath.'

After a while I stop shivering and gasping for breath, and it feels like I'm floating. I want to smile because it feels warm. Stroking my skin, comforting.

'Add some hot water. Hurry up.'

Mmm, I could stay in here for ever.

'Put her head under.'

It feels so nice; like I can relax and breathe under the water.

'Get her out, you dumb bitch. She's drowning.'

'You'd better phone your mother. She'll know what to do.'

Patti must have appeared at the bathroom door, because Mom is yelling at her to get out.

I try to smile at my little sister and tell her I'm okay, but it comes out wrong. 'I'm going to see my brothers.'

'Stop crying, Patti, and get out.'

'But what's she talking about, Mom?'

'California,' I whisper. 'They're in California.'

My stepdad's whining down the phone. 'I swear we never hurt her on purpose, Mom. She just wouldn't do as she was told. Kids need discipline, don't they? Okay, Mom. Bye.'

Mom is slapping my face. 'Help me clean her up, Richard. Come on, don't just stand there, help me.'

'We need to get her to a hospital, Angie.'

'You think I want to go to jail? Oh God, let's just bury her, Richard.'

'We can't do that! I'm calling 911, honey. If I don't, my mom's gonna.'

I've never known them to be so scared. But I'm not. Not anymore. And something's missing. The pain! There's no pain. I've lived with it so long it feels weird without it. And I just know I'm getting out of here. I'll be on my way to California soon.

Sirens.

But it all still seems so far away.

'Oh, dear God.' One of the paramedics throws up on Mom's bathroom carpet. I'll be blamed for that, but I don't care.

Another one lifts me up. 'Is she still breathing?'

Of course I am. I've never breathed so easy in my entire life.

'Get her out of this shit-hole, Ryan. And there's another two kids in the kitchen. Hey, don't let the parents out of your sight.'

More sirens. The cops this time. They pass me and Ryan in the front hall.

'What the hell?' says one.

I'm floating. It's just like in my stories. The one where God comes for me and I'm carried away to Heaven. Oh, it's peaceful.

I can tell when we get to the hospital because they kill the siren and I'm being rushed down a long corridor. I want to ask them to slow down, that everything's alright now. Strip lights flash above my head.

'She's going. Hey, stay with us, sweetheart. Stay with us.'

I'm not staying though. I'm going. I'm going to California or to Heaven, and I don't care which. It feels wonderful. And it's over.

An Overview of Jeanette's Case

Jeanette Marie Maples

09.08.94 - 09.12.09

aged 15 years & 4 months

Eugene, Oregon, USA

At her death, Jeanette weighed just 50lbs and she had more than 200 wounds on her body, most of them infected; some right down to the bone. Her mother had used a knife in an attempt to cut out the dying flesh. The dog faeces she and her sister had been forced to collect and then had rubbed into her face obscured her battered features.

Her body was criss-crossed with welts from the many whippings she'd had to endure when she couldn't obey her mother's command to stand perfectly still with her arms in the air for hours at a time. Her lips were pulverised due to incessant battering with shoes, and her teeth were broken down to the gums.

She had pneumonia caused by an abscessed lung, and bleeding on the brain due to a massive head injury. A few days before the murder, Angela McAnulty had pointed out a wound on the back of Jeanette's head to her other daughter, Patti, saying 'If someone was stabbed in the back of the head with a tree branch, it would cause brain damage'. By that time, Jeanette was incoherent and confused; asking for a blanket when she was already covered by it. Two belts, stiff with blood, and a number of red-stained tree branches were found at the scene.

Jeanette had so many injuries, inflicted in so many ways, that it was impossible to say what had killed her.

§

Jeanette's mother's childhood was traumatic. She was born Angela Darlene Feusi on 2 October 1968, into a home with issues of abuse and infidelity. When Angela was five, her mother Nancy left the family home, and went to live in a hotel room with her five children. One night, she went out dancing and never came back. When her dead body was later found, Nancy had been stabbed 29 times. Her killer was never brought to justice, and for a time, her husband was under suspicion. The children spent time in foster care, before being returned to their father and new stepmother. Angela's brothers, Mike and George, reported that the home, which now housed eight children, ran under strict rules. All the children were beaten with a belt, and they were not allowed to take food from the kitchen when they were hungry, although they were permitted to take water from the tap.

When Angela was sixteen, she left home to travel with a carnival worker, and became involved with drugs. She subsequently met and married Anthony Maples, and gave birth to two boys and Jeanette. When both parents were jailed for drug offences, the three children were taken into care. Jeanette was one year old.

Six years later, when the matter of returning the children was being discussed, the two young boys wrote to the judge, begging not to be returned to their mother. The judge granted their request, but the seven year old little girl was made to go back to her. By this time, Jeanette had a new half-sister, with whom she formed a close bond. Angela soon met truck driver, Richard McAnulty, and they married in 2002. They had a son, and in 2006 the family moved from California to Oregon, Richard's home state.

By this time, the abuse had already begun, with Jeanette being denied food and water, and being terrified of going home after the school-day was over. A school cafeteria worker, Michelle Mullins, stated that when she noticed how thin the girl was getting, she would feed her extra food in the lunch break, as Jeanette's mother was only packing a piece of cheese and one cracker in her daughter's lunch-box. After a while, a tearful Jeanette told the worker she couldn't accept the food anymore, as her mother had noticed that she was gaining weight and was punishing her for it. Mullins later testified in court that she reported the situation to the child protection services. An investigation took place, but the case was soon closed, with no action taken, after McAnulty informed the agency that her daughter was a compulsive liar and not to be trusted.

In May 2008, when her daughter's skinny and unkempt appearance led to more reports being made to the Department of Human Services, Jeanette's mother took her out of school, allegedly to be 'homeschooled'. Now she could be tortured out of sight of those who were trying to save her. Eighteen months of living hell later, Jeanette was dead.

§

Jeanette's stepfather, Richard McAnulty, was a long distance truck driver who was sometimes away from home for weeks at a time. In July 2009, he suffered a major heart attack, and subsequent complications required further hospital admissions. These included an infected catheter site, which caused intermittent loss of consciousness and profuse bleeding. Due to his ill-health, Richard McAnulty was spending more time at home, and he claims it was only from this point onwards that he became aware of the extent to which his elder stepdaughter was being cruelly 'punished' by her mother.

A short time before her death, Jeanette showed her stepfather her injuries, and the blood spattered back bedroom in which she was tortured. Richard did not act to help Jeanette, but instead enforced his wife's decision to restrict the child's food and water intake.

He pleaded guilty to murder by abuse for failing to prevent or report Jeanette's torture.

Jeanette's younger sister gave evidence at her mother's trial, saying that she had been warned not to reveal anything to the authorities about her sister's condition. She was told on a daily basis, 'What happens in the house, stays in the house', and she had therefore told investigators that Jeanette was fine. McAnulty met any attempts to help Jeanette with further beatings.

§

Jeanette's mother, Angela Darlene McAnulty, is now on death row for the murder of her daughter, and her stepfather, Richard McAnulty, was sentenced to life in prison with no chance of parole until he has served twenty five years.

Following the trials, a sealed affidavit filed on the day after Jeanette's death was deemed fit to be opened, as it would no longer pose a threat to the fairness of the court proceedings. It gave additional information not included in the trial, including a statement by Jeanette's five year old half-brother, who demonstrated to a caseworker how his mother used to hit his sister. In his own words: 'She hits hard, and I mean hard. It makes a swooshing sound, and that gives me a headache all day.'

In a classic example of understatement, so often exhibited by child torture/killers, Angela McAnulty said: 'I did wrong. I should never have spanked my daughter with a belt.'

Public reaction to Jeanette's death includes criticisms of various family members, including the two brothers who escaped their mother's home and cruelty, and Richard's mother Lynn McAnulty. As outsiders, we have the overwhelming benefit of hindsight and it is easy to judge when we are so appalled at the little girl's dreadful fate.

Jeanette's older brothers were children when they were taken out of the family home and still children when they asked not to be returned. Were they responsible for not being able to save Jeanette? I am sure they live with terrible guilt for escaping the same fate as their little sister, and wish they could have saved her. But in view of the fact that child protection services were told about the torture and failed to save Jeanette, what success could two abused little boys have had?

Lynn McAnulty, Jeanette's step-grandmother, was horrified at the injuries she saw on the child, and rang Children's Services at least four times. She is criticised for calling anonymously. But should she have given her name and run the risk of losing all contact with her grandchildren, and the opportunities to check on them?

Another concerned family member, Richard McAnulty's cousin Mary, was perhaps not the only one who offered to take Jeanette and look after her. Perhaps they had to look on helplessly as Jeanette's condition deteriorated, and her mother's abuse increased.

The paid professionals who missed several chances to appropriately follow up not only on Lynn's calls, but on those of Jeanette's school friends and teachers, are easy targets for our frustration. But we are all wise after the event. And most of us do not know how we ourselves would have acted if we had known Jeanette personally; perhaps we too would have been deceived by her torturer's obscuring of the facts. Perhaps.

Once Jeanette was removed from school, her torture could continue unabated. There is a long-running heated discussion about homeschooling children, and I refer to it in a little detail at the end of this book. I am not against homeschooling per se. But I support the Coalition for Responsible Home Education, which advocates exactly that – *responsibility*. What horrifies me, however, is that when an abusive parent comes under scrutiny, they are able to remove the child from sight and torture them with impunity.

There is a lovely tribute to Jeanette on YouTube; a simple montage of photographs, posted by her cousin, showing those of us who never knew her that she was a beautiful girl, who was quiet and loved school, and liked to write poetry.

**My thanks to Clare from the UK
for suggesting Jeanette's story.**

Rest Safely in Peace, Jeanette

The Homeschool Debate

An increasing number of parents are homeschooling their children, in order to offer them a better education in a safe, bully-free environment, well suited to the child's needs. I was happily homeschooled myself for a short while.

Tragically, some homeschooled children, like Jeanette, do not have caring parents. Instead, the caregiver removes the child from school when evidence of abuse (such as bruises or a change in the child's behaviour) has been spotted by school-friends or teachers.

With lamentably few safeguards in place, abusive parents can isolate the children, and, hidden from view, increase the starvation and torture they have already begun, with some eventually murdering the child in their care.

> ***To be absolutely clear: I am not criticising homeschooling parents across the board. There are some wonderful ones, who homeschool successfully, putting their children first.***

Some of the potential dangers could be addressed with relative ease. Whilst nurturing parents would welcome support from an education body, who, in addition to ensuring an acceptable environment and level of education, could regularly speak to the child in private.

Abusive parents who attempt to block these simple measures, by refusing to answer the door to the authorities, could be looked at more closely. The parents may also present a façade of learning by having a couple of books handy, and then escalating the abuse as soon as the door is closed. But if suspicions are raised, these situations could be followed up, and the child protected.

If the home environment is found to be neither suitable nor safe, the children should be returned to school, with further checks made on their care.

For more information on responsible homeschooling, check out the Coalition for Responsible Home Education —CHRE. They state: "While there are homeschooled children who experience a positive, child-centred learning environment at home, this is not always the case. Some parents take advantage of states' minimal homeschooling laws to isolate or abuse children."

Fit For A Mother's Love

'Hi, Mrs Dickinson. Just take a seat.'

'Thanks, Sara-Jayne. Do you think I'll have long to wait? He's in a really bad way again.'

'No, not long. There's just two in front of you.'

The dark-haired woman leans into the window. 'Any chance of us jumping the queue, Sara-Jayne? He's been drowsy like this all morning.'

The six-year-old's head is lolling onto his chest, arms hanging limp over the sides of his wheelchair.

Sara-Jayne checks the waiting room. 'Go and wait round the corner,' she says in a half-whisper. 'Then you can nip in when you see the patient come out.'

I look up from filling out a maternity form. 'Poor woman looks worried out of her mind.'

'Yeah,' says Sara-Jayne. 'It's really sad. I can remember Michael when he was running around with his brother and sister.'

'What happened?'

'Well, it must be at least three years ago now ...'

The main door bursts open and a young mum and her two children are blown in. She lets her brolly drip all over the floor.

Sara-Jayne purses her lips. 'Hello, Janice.'

'Hi, Sara-Jayne. Oh, we got a new girl?' Her stale breath gusts into my face.

'Yeah. Hi, I'm Alison.'

The children's knees are grubby and scabbed, and they must've grown out of those clothes months ago. They're bickering over a sherbet fountain.

Their mother whirls round. 'What did I tell you?'

'Sorry, Mam,' they chorus, with sticky grins. The girl wipes her snotty nose on her sleeve.

Janice turns back to the window. 'So Alison, what brings you here to the wilds of Cumbria?'

I frown. 'Bit of a long story really. I'm waiting to re-start my nurse training in Newcastle in September. Just earning a bit of cash to tide me over.'

'Good for you! Hope you enjoy it. Most of the locals don't bite!'

'Oh! Well, thanks!'

'So, d'you think I could see somebody? I still haven't got rid of this bloody cough.'

'Take a seat, Janice,' says Sara-Jayne. 'I'll see what I can do.' She rolls her eyes at me as she pulls the window closed. 'Talk about chalk and cheese. All she's bothered about is her flippin' smokers' cough, and there's poor Michelle Dickinson ...'

'It's a shame we can't choose our parents,' I say, watching Janice and her kids play havoc with the toys in the children's corner. 'You wonder whether those two really stand a chance. But anyway, you were going to tell me what happened to little Michael?'

'Oh, yes. Severe epilepsy. He fits almost constantly now. They can't seem to control it.'

'Aww, that's tough. He's such a bonny little fella too.'

The doctor buzzes through. 'Sara-Jayne, can you nip to the chemist's for me? It'll be a lot easier than Mrs Dickinson going there with Michael.'

'Yes, of course. I'll pop in now for the prescription.' She's back out of the doctor's room in no time, wafting the green slip of paper. 'Wow,' she says. 'He's had to increase the dose again. Poor little lad's already on about double the usual.'

'Says Dr Sara-Jayne!'

She laughs. 'See you in a bit, Alison. You'll be alright, won't you?' She's looking meaningfully over at Janice and her kids.

'Oh God, yeah. I'll be fine.'

'Oh, and you can call the next patient. Mrs D's on her way back round.'

Michelle parks her son's wheelchair in front of the window.

'You both look worn out,' I say, smiling at the little boy. Although he's drooling a little, you can tell he's been a cute kid. 'I love your haircut, Michael.'

He bobs his head and moves his hand; it almost looks like he's giving me the thumbs up.

Michelle crosses her arms and rests them on the counter. 'He can't understand you. Can you, son?'

'What a shame, he's such a lovely lad. Bet he keeps you busy.'

'You're not kidding. But you just have to keep going.'

'Has he been ill for a long time?'

'Oh God, yeah. All his life really. He was born premature and was in an incubator for a while, and then it turned out he had asthma as well,' says Michelle. 'But this, this has been going on for nearly four years. Since he was three.'

'Aww, poor little thing. Sara-Jayne was saying she can remember him running about the place.'

'Well, he's never *really* been well. And he probably won't get better now.'

'Oh, I'm so sorry.'

'Yeah, he's too ill to go school anymore, bless him. It's hard, but we struggle on.'

I'm not sure what else to say. 'Mmm, can't be easy.'

'He's seen specialists all over the place. They've never seen such a severe case. It's been quite dramatic at times; rushing him to hospital in the middle of the night …'

The outer door opens again, and Michelle groans at the sight of a neatly dressed older woman. 'And here comes the granny from hell.'

'Oh, what a surprise,' says the new arrival to Michelle. 'I might've known you'd be here.'

The woman is brisk, though not unpleasant, as she checks in for her own appointment.

'Another M Dickinson,' I smile. 'That's three of you on my first day!'

'I thought I hadn't seen you before,' she says. 'Nice to meet you. You can just call me Margaret.' She turns to her grandson and I'm sure I see him try to smile. She crouches down beside him and strokes his hair. He struggles to turn himself round to face her, and she kisses him.

'Come to cause trouble again, have you?' says her daughter-in-law.

'You know I don't want trouble, Michelle.' Her tone is much softer now, wistful. 'I just wish you'd let me see my grandchildren more. I could help you. Especially with Michael.' She takes her grandson's hand and squeezes it. 'Couldn't I, Michael?'

'Yeah, like I'm going to let you keep poking your nose in,' says Michelle.

I'm relieved when Sara-Jayne returns from the chemist's.

Margaret bristles again. 'What's that? More drugs?'

Michelle shakes her head. 'It's med-i-cine, as you well know. To help my son.' She turns Michael's wheelchair round, and he murmurs as she wheels him out of the building.

Mrs Dickinson senior purses her lips. 'That woman! Oh, I'm sorry, girls.'

'It's okay,' I say, relieved she's not my mother-in-law.

As we're finishing for the day, Sara-Jayne can't wait to fill me in on the Dickinson family. 'It's a scandal really. Silly old woman reckons Michael doesn't have epilepsy at all, and Michelle's drugging him up to the eyeballs for the heck of it!'

'Eh?'

'I know, bonkers isn't it? If she had her way the poor little fella probably wouldn't be on any medication at all!'

'Where do people get these ideas from? Surely that would be really dangerous for Michael.'

'It used to give me sleepless nights when I first heard about it. But thank God, no-one seems to be listening to her.'

'Oh my God, yeah.'

'It's a nightmare for Michelle. Wouldn't you have thought Margaret would support Michael and his mam? But she keeps trying to put Michelle in the wrong, so she has to waste time fighting her, as well as fighting to help Michael.' Sara-Jayne sighs. 'And to cap it all, Michael's big sister has epilepsy too, and I think his little brother's starting with it as well.'

'Oh, my God. So it runs in families. I never knew that. That poor woman.'

The last patient gives us a wave on his way out.

'Phew, what a day,' says Sara-Jayne. 'How have you found it?'

'It's been really good. And thanks for showing me what to do.'

'No probs.' Sara-Jayne clicks the kettle on. 'Hey, what's this long story you mentioned earlier on? About how you ended up in our little village?'

I've been dreading her bringing it up again. 'I had to drop out of my nurse's training in my final year.'

'How come? Oh, sorry; only if you don't mind telling me.'

I don't mind telling her part of it. 'I got pregnant.'

'Oh, honey. Is that good or bad?'

So bad you wouldn't believe.

'Good, mostly. I've got a little boy. He's four months old now.' *Oh God, I'm filling up.*

'Hey, Alison. Are you okay?'

'Yes. Yeah, I'm fine. It's just hard sometimes, y'know. I'm on my own.'

'Father didn't want to know?'

'Something like that.' *Father doesn't know. Will never know.*

'But a little boy. Aww, that must be wonderful.'

It would be, Sara-Jayne, if he wasn't the result of that slimy creep raping me. 'Yeah, he's the best,' I say, dreading picking him up after work and spending yet another night trying not to smack him.

We're just checking all the windows are locked when we hear a frantic banging on the door.

'Just ignore it,' says Sara-Jayne. 'They know the surgery hours, and they should have the number for the on-call doctor.'

The banging continues. 'Let me in. It's urgent.'

Sara-Jayne sighs. 'Better open it, I suppose. We don't want anything drastic to happen, and then get the blame for it!'

Janice practically falls into the room. I can hear the kids outside, coughing.

'Oh, thank God,' she says, making for the children's corner. She grabs something from under the plastic bricks and holds it up in triumph. 'You saved my life, Sara-Jayne. Can't do without my ciggies.'

My second day at the surgery is remarkably similar to the first. A worried Michelle brings Michael in because he's in a worse state than yesterday. And Janice seems to be in a foul mood when she bursts in with her kids. All three of them cough their germs around the waiting room, as I try to fit them in to see Dr Walker. Out of the corner of my eye, I watch her laying down the law with the kids, before she stomps out, cigarette in hand, leaving them looking listlessly at the jigsaws and bricks. They're much quieter than yesterday, and I'm sure the boy has the beginnings of a black eye.

I nudge Sara-Jayne. 'Is that what I think it is?'

'Oh, not again. Those kids always seem bruised or scratched to hell these days.'

I give her a meaningful look.

'I know, I know. And I think it started around the time the new boyfriend appeared on the scene.'

'Well, something's going on, Sara-Jayne.'

'I try not to interfere. It's probably nothing.'

'Yes, but ...'

Janice storms back in. 'Get here, you two. We can't wait here all day. I've got a cough bottle from next door.' And out she goes without a backward glance or a thank you to me for overhauling the entire day's appointment schedule.

The next few weeks fly by. I get to know 'the regulars', the doctors are friendly and fair, and I get along well with Sara-Jayne. And I develop a real soft spot for Michael. I'm sure he starts to recognise me, and when I squat down by his side and chat to him, he reaches for my hand. Though understandably, Michelle is protective of him, and usually puts herself between us.

'I think he was trying to talk to me, Michelle.'

'It looks like that sometimes, but he isn't really. He can't speak anymore, Alison. I only wish he could.'

'Do you want to take a seat, Michelle?' says Sara-Jayne. 'You must be exhausted.'

'No, thanks. I'm alright here, talking to you. Mind, you're right. It *is* tiring. But I don't need to rest. I'd do anything for my kids. They're my world.'

The doctor buzzes through.

'That's you now, Michelle.'

I'm back doing my nurse training and doing really well this time. I don't even mind being back in Newcastle. It's amazing how things have changed for me over the past few months. It hasn't always been easy, especially with Rob, my new partner, out of work, but at least he's been able to look after Keiron.

I'm in the staff canteen, trying to persuade the ancient coffee machine to deliver something hot and wet, when someone taps me on the back.

'It's Alison, isn't it? From the doctor's surgery?'

'Yes, hi. How are you?' I know her face but I can't quite place her.

'Struggling on. He's had to be admitted today. They think he's got pneumonia now.'

The penny drops. Mrs Dickinson. 'Oh, I'm sorry to hear that, Michelle. Can't they treat him nearer to home?'

'Oh no! He's far too poorly for that.'

'Where is he now?'

'They've taken him to the ICU.'

'Well, I'd better let you get back up there. I hope he gets better soon, Michelle.'

She shakes her head. 'It's highly unlikely, Alison. I don't think he'll pull through this time.'

'Oh, Michelle. I'm so sorry.'

Her eyes are shining. 'It's been a terrible day. His nasogastric tube got bent and everything went into his lungs instead of his stomach. That's why we've had to dash through here.'

I can feel myself going pale. 'How on earth did that happen?'

She shrugs. 'Just one of those things. But yeah, his fluids and medication all went down the wrong way, down his wind-pipe, and straight into his lungs. So now we're left in this situation.'

'That's awful. Someone's made a dreadful mistake there, Michelle. But listen, you'll want to get back to him and I need to get back on my ward.'

She rests her hand on my arm. 'He's in good hands, Alison. But I think he'll have to be transferred for specialist care. There's a unit down in Leicester.'

'I'm sorry.'

'They don't expect him to make it. They've told me that. But they have to try everything.'

I can only nod in sympathy.

'Having sick children is just the worst thing ever. I can't tell you how many tests he's had. And don't get me started on the medication he has to take.'

'I really have to go now, Michelle. It was nice to see you, and good luck.' I almost have to prise her off me so I can get back to work.

My friend Ash and I are in the lunch-time queue a few days later, when two junior doctors come into the cafeteria, supporting a patient who can barely walk. A second glance shows me I'm mistaken; the ashen-faced woman isn't a patient after all.

'Oh no! Poor Michelle.'

'You know her?'

'It's her son. I think he must've died.'

'Alison! Oh, Alison!' She staggers over to me, sobbing. 'There's no hope. They've tried everything.'

'Is he? ...'

'Not yet. But he's got to go to Leicester.'

One of the doctors is still at her side. 'There's still a good chance he'll recover, Mrs Dickinson. It's the best place for him.'

'I'm sure you're right. But they won't have treated anyone as sick as Michael before.'

'I'm so sorry, Michelle.'

She gathers herself together. 'I can do this. I've been through so much already.'

I pat her arm. 'You can. You have to be strong for Michael.'

'They need to let me help him. But *she's* trying to interfere again. You know who I mean, Alison. You've seen her in action. I'm his mother, for God's sake.'

'Come and sit down, Michelle,' says the doctor. 'You're dead on your feet.'

'I don't sleep, Alison. I have to be there for him day and night.'

The doctor leads her away. 'You need to trust us, Mrs Dickinson. The consultant knows what he's doing.'

Rob looks up from his paper. He's still out of work, but since I got my promotion a few months ago we've been doing okay. I miss the friendliness of the wards though.

'Had a good day, Ali-babes?'

'Yeah, not bad. But I'm shattered.'

'Hey, this'll interest you. There's a news article here from where you used to work.'

The last thing I want to think about is work. By the state of Keiron, Rob hasn't cleaned him up properly since making chocolate brownies this afternoon. I need to sort him out, then think about tea. 'Mmm, okay Rob. Tell me later, alright?' It feels good to kick off my shoes.

'It's about a patient from that village in Cumbria.'

I don't say anything. Perhaps he'll leave it. I grab a wet cloth and make a start on Keiron's sticky face. He grins at me and I smile back.

'I've never heard anything like it.'

He's obviously determined to tell me.

'Go on, then. What's it about?'

'Says a mother slowly poisoned her own child, pretended he had epilepsy. Fooled the doctors and everybody.'

'Oh yeah?' The chocolate is pretty much caked on, and I have to rub harder.

'They reckon it's one of those Münchausen's things.'

'Münchausen's, eh? Rob, couldn't you at least have wiped Keiron's hands and face?'

'Sorry, love. Anyway, she tried to poison her other kids too.'

Kieron screws up his face and I realise I'm squeezing his arm too tightly. I let go and tell him to go and play.

'And it's from where I worked just before we met?'

Rob nods. 'Only the grandmother suspected her, but nobody would listen. Hey, what's up love? You've gone all white.'

I swallow hard and turn to Rob. 'Michael. It's Michael, isn't it?'

An Overview of Michael's Case

Michael Dickinson

18.02.93 - 14.10.00

aged 7 years & 8 months

West Cumbria, England

Michael was the middle child of three, a premature baby, who needed special care following his birth. From the time he was three years old, his mother, Michelle Dickinson, informed her GP that her son was experiencing *absences*, a mild form of seizure, formerly known as *petit mal*. When she reported that the seizures were becoming more severe and more frequent, Michael's treatment for epilepsy began.

The dosage of medication administered to Michael increased over time, and in addition, his mother obtained repeat prescriptions more and more often. But Michael's condition worsened.

Between late 1997 and early 1998, a specialist teacher noted that Michael was deteriorating from a fully mobile and conversant little boy, to one who could not walk or talk.

Michael's paternal grandmother, Margaret, first tried to alert the authorities in 1998, two years before Michael died, as she suspected that her daughter-in-law was intentionally harming her children. She hoped that, at the very least, Michelle herself could be offered support. However, Margaret's voice went unheard, with social workers accusing her of 'interfering'.

In early 1999, Michael's mother, and also teaching staff, were administering medication, including rectal diazepam, at the school he attended. Around this time, his mother falsely informed staff that Michael had Lennox Gastaut Syndrome and that it was a terminal illness. (The medical profession are still learning about LGS, and whilst the syndrome itself is not fatal, the increase in sudden seizures can cause falls, which may result in severe injury or death). She also told a relative that the GP had said they could 'do no more for Michael'.

§

When Michael was admitted for tests to Newcastle General Hospital in January 2000, the results showed no evidence of the symptoms reported by his mother. Consultant Paediatric Neurologist, Dr Ramesh, was of the opinion that Michael's deterioration was caused by phenytoin toxicity, and recommended that he should be gradually weaned off phenytoin, and another of the many drugs he was taking. Michael was also fitted with a temporary nasogastric tube, to allow his food and medication to pass directly into his stomach.

By March 2000, Michael was again being administered a cocktail of drugs in double the recommended dosages, and was suffering from confusion, memory loss and erratic sleep patterns. He was seen by Dr Richard Appleton, at Alder Hey Hospital in Liverpool, who was keen to admit Michael as an in-patient, to get to the bottom of his symptoms, but his mother did not allow this to take place, perhaps fearing that her actions would be discovered.

On the morning of 26 June 2000 – the day that Michael was due to be admitted for more tests to try and get to the bottom of his inexplicable symptoms – his mother made an urgent call to the GP to say that he was having difficulty breathing. She was instructed not to administer any more drugs and was told that Michael would be urgently admitted to his local hospital. Michelle Dickinson ignored this instruction. In the ambulance on the way to the hospital, she administered medication via the nasogastric tube which mysteriously doubled back, causing drugs and food to pass into the wind-pipe and lungs instead of the stomach. Michael was soon transferred to Newcastle-upon-Tyne and then to Glenfield Hospital in Leicester to receive specialist treatment for the pneumonia caused by this damage.

Whilst an in-patient at Glenfield, Michael's feeding tube (again) malfunctioned, when his mother was present, and hospital personnel were certain that neither staff error nor equipment failure could have led to the malfunction. They also expressed the view that Michael did not suffer from epilepsy, and found that on withdrawal of all medication, no seizures were detected.

It was around this time that Michael's grandmother at last got someone to listen to her suspicions about her daughter-in-law, and the NSPCC began to look into the case, and Michael's siblings were taken into care for their own safety.

But it all came too late to save Michael. After spending the latter part of his life in a toxic confusional state, due to the administering of a cocktail of unnecessary medication at double the safe recommended dosages, and developing pneumonia as a result of the malfunction of the nasogastric tube, Michael died after 102 days on life support. One can barely imagine the physical and mental trauma the little boy endured for most of his life.

A post-mortem showed that Michael had no signs of epilepsy.

§

Michelle Dickinson had also been claiming that Michael's two siblings had the same condition. By the time Michael was admitted to hospital for the last few months of his life, Michelle was already excessively medicating his older sister, and was beginning the process with his younger brother. Once safely placed in foster care when suspicions about their mother's behaviour were finally taken seriously, Michael's sister was gradually weaned off the medication and has spent the intervening years with no symptoms. As Michael's grandmother was told by her solicitor: 'If you hadn't have done what you did, we would've been looking at three dead children'.

§

Michelle Dickinson was tried at Liverpool Crown Court, and was cleared of the charge of murder, as it could not be proven that her actions in the ambulance led to Michael's death. On 22nd July 2002, she was convicted of attempted murder and various counts of child cruelty.

Detective Superintendent Jon Rush, who led the investigation, was hopeful that Dickinson would never again be in a position of power over children or other vulnerable people.

On 13th January 2003, Michelle Dickinson was sentenced to life; a term of sixteen years, with a minimum of eight years and four months before parole would be considered.

Justice Pitchers was in no doubt that Dickinson's crime could not be seen as simply the result of mental illness, and that she was clearly a perpetrator of child abuse. 'You did choose to do all the dreadful things you did. I regard this sort of behaviour as absolutely at the top of the scale of cruelty to children.'

On 8th June 2004, Michelle Dickinson appealed against the attempted murder conviction, on the grounds that it was unsafe, with the judge having misdirected the jury. Although the appeal was successful, her sentence was unchanged, due to the conviction for child cruelty. Dickinson served her sentence first at Durham, then at Styal Women's Prison near Manchester. She was denied parole on two occasions before her release.

§

The term Münchausen's Syndrome by Proxy was first used in the 1970's to describe the actions of a caregiver who deliberately harms the child in their care, whilst presenting as a loving parent. The syndrome is now known in the UK as FII – Fabricated or Induced Illness, but as most people still know it as Münchausen's

Syndrome by Proxy, I will use MSBP, the better known acronym. MSBP covers a wide range of abuses, including subjecting the child to unnecessary operations, invasive tests, excessive medication, overdosing with salt, adding blood, sugar, urine and faecal matter to samples to give false readings, and tampering with equipment.

Rapper Eminem has spoken of MSBP in his family, reporting that his mother repeatedly took him to medical appointments for symptoms he did not have, and that when the syndrome was discovered, he was awarded custody of his younger brother.

MSBP remains one of the most complex categories of child abuse. The harming parent breaks the bargain that is implicitly made when they take a child to the doctor, ie that they want the child to be checked over and be relieved of their symptoms, and/or be cured of an illness. The doctor usually believes the parent, and tries to use their skills to help the child. However, a child caught up in the web of MSBP was not actually ill in the first place, and the parent does not want the child to recover. One of the tragic elements of MSBP is that a doctor, in an effort to relieve the child of its reported symptoms, unwittingly colludes with the parent to harm the child.

As a society, we are loath to confront the fact that a mother, particularly one who presents as caring deeply for her children, and appears to be doing all she can to ensure they receive the best of medical attention, could intentionally induce symptoms in her child. Accusing such a mother seems preposterous, and even when the evidence is clear, it may be met with resistance and disbelief by other medical professionals and the perpetrator's family, with the accusation turned upon the reporter of the abuse, instead of the actual perpetrator.

The debate still rages around whether MSBP should be regarded as a psychiatric illness or child abuse (I imagine it is a combination of the two) and indeed whether it exists at all; some dissenters attributing a child's repeated symptoms to rare or as yet undiscovered conditions.

On a (thankfully small) number of discussion threads on the internet, I have seen a regrettable and baffling crossover between SIDS (Sudden Infant Death Syndrome) and MSBP, and parents whose children have fallen victim to SIDS should not be made to suffer further pain following the tragic death of a child. The clue to the difference is surely in the name. There is nothing sudden about the vast majority of deaths of the children of MSBP parents. The parent seeks the drama, attention and sense of importance that presenting themselves as a devoted and courageous caregiver brings. They are happy to attend appointment after appointment, lending their own 'expertise' to the troubling symptoms exhibited by the unfortunate victim, and glorying in the various tests and procedures carried out. Death only occurs when there is nowhere else to go; when the excess of medication finally kills the child, or when the parent's abuse is on the brink of being found out, and they react with panic and desperation, as Michelle Dickinson is suspected to have done in the ambulance with Michael.

§

The exception to this pattern is Nurse Beverley Allitt (and other so-called 'Angels of Death') who murdered four children in her care, and caused harm (in some cases irrevocable) to nine others. However, this exception can be explained by the constant stream of victims available to Allitt – she could therefore afford to murder each one fairly quickly, as there would always be a new admission to the ward whose life and suffering she could manipulate.

Allitt came from an unremarkable background and, as a child, would gain attention by wearing bandages over non-existent injuries. Over the years, she exhibited classic signs of Münchausen's Syndrome, complaining of many illnesses, some of which rewarded her with hospital admissions, including undergoing an appendectomy on a healthy appendix. When she secured a position at the local hospital, she found that nurses were held in high esteem by patients' families; even more so when a child became seriously ill, and she selflessly offered to watch over them. This afforded her the opportunities to harm the young patient, and by graduating from Münchausen's Syndrome to Münchausen's by Proxy, Allitt had found her niche.

Added in September 2023, following the sentencing of children's nurse, Lucy Letby, who murdered seven babies in her place of employment on the neonatal ward at the Countess of Chester hospital in the UK.

There is currently a debate as to whether Letby was an MSBP murderer. Being alert to the possibility several months ago, I mooted the idea on Facebook and provoked some ridicule. (Though the ridicule was by no means universal.) We now have a number of psychiatrists coming forward with this theory. There is still precious little known about the 'syndrome' and some are averse to the label as they fear it reduces the guilt of the murderer. It remains to be seen whether Letby falls into this category, but I feel it is worth considering.

§

Michael's death prompted a Serious Case Review, undertaken by Cumbria Child Protection Committee, and the resulting public report states: 'In this case, Michael's paternal grandmother deserves special mention. She felt there was something 'not right' about Michael's situation and tried to draw this to the attention of various agencies.

Unfortunately, on her first contact, the significance of her information was not recognised. She made further representations after Michael was admitted to hospital for the last time. Although those representations did not save Michael's life, they were important in contributing to the knowledge and understanding of this family.' Perhaps they *could* have saved Michael's life, had her representations been listened to and believed at the appropriate time.

The report also makes a recommendation repeated time and again in cases of child torture: 'Communication (or the lack of it), the failure to identify information as of sufficient importance and the failure to share information is a continuing theme in cases of child abuse. Any individual who has information that suggests something about the situation of the child is 'not right' must be empowered to make their voice heard.'

§

Michael's grandmother embodies my ABCD of child abuse detection:

Assume Nothing

Be Vigilant

Check Everything

Do Something.

But it also demonstrates that even following this mantra is no guarantee that the child's life will be saved.

It is of course true that non-abusive parents may attend clinics with their child on a frequent basis, with genuine concerns about their health. (In a further complication to this already complex situation, it should not be forgotten that clinicians are capable of being negligent or incompetent, in which case a worried parent may be forced into making frequent requests to have their child attended to.)

However, Page 9 of the Serious Case Review report examines what professionals should do if they suspect MSBP, advising that this avenue should be explored if, when given a plausible explanation for the child's symptoms, a parent does not express relief, but instead re-emphasises the problem or presents new evidence to support her belief that the child is ill: 'The worrying parent will be supported and reassured. The harming parent will break out of any containment strategy'.

On page 10 of the report, the writers urge those involved in such a case not to focus on the delusions of the parent: 'To protect children, we must concentrate on assessing harm to the child, rather than trying to understand something which is not rational.'

The report is a thorough and enlightening piece of work on the subject of MSBP, and to the best of my knowledge, was the first report of its kind in the UK.

In her book 'Parents Who Kill', author Carol Anne Davis quotes from a discussion she had with Dr Marc Feldman, a leading expert in MSBP: 'Many of the perpetrators seem to have disengaged from the children they abused, treating them as objects to be manipulated rather than individuals to be nurtured.'

This is surely true of most, if not all, of the murderers in this collection.

My thanks to Margaret from the UK for her support in my writing of her grandson's story.

Rest Safely in Peace, Michael

Who's To Blame?

Michael's grandmother appealed many times to social services to investigate the actions of her daughter-in-law towards her children.

She is not the only family member to spot abuse and repeatedly beg the authorities to listen and intervene. When their pleas go unheard, and a child is murdered, the heart-break, frustration and fury must be all but unbearable.

These instances of negligence by the authorities have understandably led to suspicion and anger. Children's Services are often blamed for the child's death, sometimes with an individual social worker being singled out and scapegoated. Without doubt, this may be appropriate on occasion, and it is easy to see why bereaved families might focus on the shortcomings of those who are paid to safeguard society's children.

When the shock and disbelief of another child murder fade, we move onto anger and blame. Sadly, we often stay stuck in this stage, expending our energy on outrage, instead of channelling it into searching for answers that could prevent the next child from being tortured to death.

To break out of this vicious circle, where we see only evil monsters and woefully incompetent agencies, we need to look past our fury to find out *why the torture happens in the first place*.

The aim is ***not*** to excuse the abusers' behaviour, but to learn how to prevent the behaviour from happening, and save children.

In their book Beyond Blame, Reder, Duncan and Gray studied 35 major public inquiries into child abuse murders in the UK, viewing each murder in a wider context.

Their most pertinent finding was that ***the caregivers' own childhood needs were not met***, so that when they eventually become caregivers themselves, if overwhelmed by the demands placed upon them, they look to the child to *fulfil their needs*. This can only end in failure, as a baby or child is *dependent* and cannot be *dependable*. Lashing out at the child who they feel has failed them, if their frustration and fury continue to build, it can culminate in extreme violence and murder.

To these caregivers, the challenges of parenting are overpowering. Gritting one's teeth, sounding off to a loved one, and begging a friend to take the baby and give them a break, are perfectly normal reactions.

But if they have no one with whom to share their frustration, if their tolerance threshold is low, or if as a child they learnt to meet stressful situations with violence, they risk venting their frustration on the child, with disastrous results.

However, I must add that when we hear of some acts of unspeakable cruelty to children, it is hard to rule out the possibility that there are truly evil people amongst us.

Blowtorch

They call me JaQuinn. It's a pretty cool name, huh?

I've got two big brothers, two big sisters, a baby sister, a mom, and a few dads. They say I'm a slow learner. I can't say all my words yet. And I can't go to the bathroom on my own. Nearly, but not quite. My big brother takes me. My big brother is the kindest person I know. He takes care of us kids when Mom's too tired. Which is most of the time.

But he wasn't around that day when one of the dads threw me around the room. I kinda bounced off the walls; my head, and everything. That's how I got to be a slow learner.

The tallest person I know is Uncle Marcus. He's 6 feet and 7 inches tall. Uncle Marcus lives with my auntie Nadera. She's Mom's friend, and also my godmother (which I think means she has to come visit me sometimes and I have to be good). It's nice when she comes to visit because she brings marshmallows and little pieces of fruit and then she takes out a little fire stick and burns them to make them go crunchy. My mom says the fire thing is a blowtorch and she says the crunchy little treats are yummy. It's good to watch it make things go crispy and brown, but it's even better when you get to try it. Once I got a piece of marshmallow that I had to share with my little sister, and another time I got a whole piece of orange to myself. I can still remember how good it tasted. I sometimes see my brothers watching the fruit go into Mom's mouth and they look like they want to make her sick it up so they can eat it. Mom sometimes does sick things up, but you wouldn't want to eat it.

So, tall Uncle Marcus. He's okay, I guess. I sat on his knee once and he was cuddling me and pinching me at the same time. I don't get cuddled much, so it was pretty nice.

I like being cuddled. My sisters used to squeeze me tight and sometimes they even kissed me. But Mom told them to stop. Said they were spoiling me. I don't want to get spoiled. But I did like it.

Most days, my big brothers and sisters go round the neighbourhood and come back with things to eat. I used to like the potato chips best. I went out with them once, and a lady gave me the choice of three flavours of chips, and when I couldn't decide between them she gave me all three. I wanted to go back the next day, but my brother said we couldn't go back too soon or she might get angry with us, so they went to a different neighbour's and brought back banana bread, and now I think that might be my new favourite thing. I never questioned my brother again. He's smart.

Sometimes Auntie Nadera brings things she's baked for Mom. I haven't tried it, but Mom says she makes the best creme brûlée in Philadelphia. And my mouth waters when I see her home-baked cookies. My big brother once pinched one off the plate and shared it out with us. Mmm, I can still taste it; sweet and crunchy. My brother got a beating when they counted up the cookies, but he said it was worth it. Mom and Auntie Nadera blamed me at first. I guess it's because I'm small and don't say much. Seems to make me easy to blame. But my brother admitted it was him. I love that guy. He told me that other kids get to eat nice stuff every day but I'm not sure about that. When I'm grown up I'm going to eat chips and cookies every day though, and give some to poor children.

We've been to a park! With swings and a slide and everything! My brother says that if we're very good we can go again next week. My baby sister didn't go because she can't walk but my brother said he'll try and carry her next time. I was a bit scared on the slide. I flew down it too fast and plopped off the end into some mud. I liked the swings better, but for that you have to wait till someone can push you. Still, it was nice just sitting in the swing and rocking backwards and forwards. But then some bigger kids came and called us nasty names and chased us off. My brother said we'll go a bit earlier next week when those other kids are in school. I asked my brother why he didn't go to school much and he just shrugged.

Mom sometimes calls me her little man. When she does we know she's in a good mood and she might cook up some rice and peas, and we won't feel hungry during the night.

But most days Mom's tired. She says us six kids drive her crazy. So she stays in bed a lot, and when she's not in bed she mostly sits on the floor in a cloud of smoke with cushions all around her. She sometimes drops off to sleep among the cushions. Then my brother has to put the fire out.

The dads come round pretty often, and they spoil Mom. They punch her in the face and say bad words. Then they take her clothes off and hurt her some more. When they hurt my sister the same way, she got sent away for a spell.

Things have gotten pretty hot around here lately, and I don't mean the fire from Mom's smokes. Or the weather. Mom can't pay the rent. You need money for that, but Mom gives all her money away to the skinny guy with the sunken cheeks who comes knocking, and he gives her a little package every time. If he doesn't come, and she doesn't get the package, Mom gets really weird and we'd all better hide. The skinny guy isn't the rent man. The rent man doesn't come through our door, and mostly when he batters on it we have to stay very quiet.

Anyway, without the rent we can't stay here, and Mom is going to a 'hostel' and us kids are either going to the hostel too, or to live with other people. It won't be for long. I don't mind because I'm going to tall Uncle Marcus' and godmother Auntie Nad's place. Just me. Mom said they mustn't spoil me, and Uncle Marcus said Oh no, they wouldn't. I was relieved.

Like a big baby, I cry when my sisters and brothers have gone, and Auntie and Uncle come for me. Auntie Nad's hand is a lot heavier than Mom's when she slaps me. And I know I have to stop crying to stop the slapping, but somehow I can't. It must be because I'm a slow learner. And suddenly I need the bathroom, and when I ask Uncle Marcus to take me, he just laughs and calls me a nasty name.

I sleep in a cot! A cot is a tiny bed and it's got a pillow and a little cover to pull up if it's cold. Auntie Nadera straps me in before they sit down for their supper and I stay there till the morning. Supper smells nice. I wet my diaper a lot during the night and they don't usually change it till it's time to go to bed again, and by then it's often dirty too. Auntie Nad doesn't like that. When she's hitting me, I try to tell her that my brother used to take me to the bathroom, and I was starting to use it like a grown-up, but I don't think she hears me. I reckon it'd be better for everyone if she just took me to the bathroom, but she's the grown-up and I'm just a kid, so maybe I've got that wrong.

My cot is getting smelly. My pillow and cover have never been washed and neither have I. Sometimes they lie me face down in the cot and I can hardly breathe, and the smell goes right in my nose and eyes and I can't sleep. My godmother has started coming to my cot during the night to check my diaper. It's always wet and dirty so she drags me out of the cot and hurts me. I'm not sure why she doesn't just sing to me and change the diaper like Mom or my brother used to. They do things a lot different here. To be honest, I don't like it here anymore. I wish my mom would come and bring my big brother, so he could show them how I could nearly use the bathroom myself. I don't know if I still can.

Now, whenever Auntie Nad or Uncle Marcus come towards me I go to the toilet on the spot. I don't like it, and neither do they.

I've had the best dream ever! My brother came and knocked at Auntie Nad's door and she let him carry me all the way downstairs and when he put me down I skipped alongside him back to our neighbourhood. As we scooted past, the potato chip lady came to her door, but my brother said we were in a hurry to get to Mom's, so she said be sure and call back and get some chips later, because she had some new flavours we might like to try. Then the banana bread lady did the same, and this time my brother took some slices and we ate a piece each and kept the rest for my mom and my brothers and sisters. Then my brother said did I want to go to the park, so I said yes and we played on the swings for a long time, until it was nearly dark. In the dream we never even got to see Mom, but we were so busy having fun, I didn't really mind.

I was sad when I woke up and I wanted to get back into the dream. But Auntie Nadera was yelling that I was a little motherfucker for soiling my diaper again and she wasn't going to stand for it.

We share the kitchen and bathroom with another family. I don't know if there's any kids, but I've seen the man a few times, and the lady just one time. The man smiled at me and said, 'Hi, little buddy. How you doin'?' I smiled back a little bit, but Auntie Nad was scowling at me, so I thought I'd better turn away. I heard him ask Auntie Nad if he could give me a Twinkie, because his mom had brought him a whole box, and I looked like the kind of little boy who could help him out. I hid my excitement as well as I could. But Auntie Nad said I couldn't have one because they didn't want to spoil me. So the man asked her if I could come by and play some time, and she said 'Sure.' I'm hoping and hoping that I can go to the man's apartment because he might let me have a Twinkie anyway. Also, I'd like to play for a while, and not just be with Auntie Nad and Uncle Marcus, who don't like me very much anymore.

Uncle Marcus is very big and strong and when he beats me, he beats me hard. It's mostly Auntie Nadera who beats me though. I can't see so well anymore, since I got punched upside the head and passed out for a while. Is this what they mean about spoiling someone? If it is, I don't like it. I don't know why they don't like me. My big brothers and sisters always said I was cute. Uncle Marcus and Auntie Nadera don't think I'm cute.

Auntie Nadera has started to whip me and I scream and she whips me for screaming and tells me to stop but I can't, so it goes on and on for a long time. I wish my big brother would come and tell her that if she stops the whipping, I'll stop the screaming. But he doesn't come. I try to protect myself but she tells me to move my hands, and calls me a motherfucker again. Sometimes she puts a sock in my mouth because she says the neighbours will hear. She turns the music up too. And one day the man from next door came, and he said that it had been going on for ages, and I don't know if he meant my screaming or the music. Auntie Nad said she'd turn it down, and she stopped the whipping too. But I got beat again the next day.

I'm frightened all the time now. I wish my big brother or my mom would come and take me home.

I've been outside today with Auntie Nad. I heard Uncle Marcus say, 'Get the little shit out of my sight' and I think he meant me. Auntie Nad cursed me too when she was trying to push my shoes onto my feet, but they've got big and swollen since she started pouring boiling water on them. It hurts a lot when she does that. I can't really walk anymore either, so she kind of dragged and carried me down the stairs and along the street. When we saw a big policeman coming towards us, Auntie Nadera quickly turned round to walk back where we'd just come from but the policeman caught up to us and asked Auntie Nad some questions. I heard him say that the little fella (that's me!) looked as if he'd been knocked about a bit, and he spoke into his radio for a while, and we had to wait. When he finished talking on the radio he said to Auntie Nad that we were 'free to go'. She dragged me along pretty quick and when we got in she told Uncle Marcus that we'd had to come back early so he needn't start anything for us messing up his afternoon.

I wish I knew what I'm being punished for, because then maybe I could stop doing it. I think it's still for wetting the bed. If it is, I can't stop it. The punishment makes me scream and scream. I could feel a fire against my bottom, and I cried out for my brother. Auntie Nad said 'He can't help you now', and the fire came again. When it stopped she put a silver thing on the table and then I could see it was the blowtorch. The thing she uses when she's making the crunchy fruit or marshmallows or the creme brûlée. But now she's using it on me, and my bottom hurts all the time from the burning and the sores and scabs. Sometimes when I scream I get punched extra hard for disturbing the neighbours, but I don't know how you can have your bottom nearly set on fire and not scream. My brother would've told them that a good way to stop me screaming would be to put the blowtorch back in the kitchen drawer, and give me a cuddle instead. They don't seem to have thought of that.

I've tried to get away. I'd decided that maybe I could find Mommy or my brother or the lady who gave us the potato chips. I don't know where I am or where they are, but perhaps I could've asked someone who looked kind.

Anyway, my plan didn't work because when I got to the door it was locked and Uncle Marcus and Auntie Nadera watched me for a while, as I struggled and cried. They weren't crying. They were laughing. Then one of them scooped me up and told me I was a bad boy, and they took turns punching me and belting me with a shoe. They said that because I'd been so naughty I deserved a special punishment that I wouldn't forget, so Auntie Nadera took out her metal hair pick and dragged it across my skin. Then they laughed and poured boiling water on my feet again and I did a lot more screaming because it hurt so much. I couldn't help it. After a while, Uncle Marcus picked me up and held me over the sink, and ran the cold faucet. When the skin peeled off my feet he tried to push it down the sink. Then he put wet cloths over my feet. He was gentle then, and it was the nicest thing to happen to me in a long time. I can't walk anymore.

So I'm just lying here. Waiting for the next punishment. If I do get to sleep I try to find a happy dream but even they've gone away, and I just have bad dreams instead, and when I wake up it's real; they're burning or whipping me again.

I can't sleep tonight and I've been trying to get out of bed, because I thought I could maybe crawl to the door and they might have left it open. But I fell over and they came and beat me so hard that I finally felt sleepy.

They said they wouldn't spoil me, but they *are* spoiling me and I don't want to be spoiled. Not like this.

JESSICA JACKSON

An Overview of JaQuinn's Case

JaQuinn Brewton

08.04.08 - 12.07.11

aged 3 years & 3 months

West Philadelphia,

Pennsylvania, USA

From at least the mid 2000's, eleven years before her son's death, JaQuinn's mother, Ashley Brewton, was struggling with addiction and with raising her children. The earliest recorded visit by social workers was in 2005, three years before JaQuinn was born, when it was said that the children were 'unsupervised and begging for food from the neighbours'.

Several other visits followed, highlighting inadequate food in the home, marijuana smoke, school non-attendance, inappropriate behaviour by the mother's boyfriend, and stating that the behaviour of one of the little girls was aggressive and sexualised. At a visit in May 2010, the safety of only three of the six children could be ascertained. Unfortunately, the agency did not follow up their findings in a timely manner, and missed several monthly visits.

For a short time, Nadera Batson, Ashley Brewton's friend of around seven years standing, and godmother to JaQuinn, resided with Brewton and her family, along with her boyfriend Marcus King. When Batson and King got their own place, and Ashley Brewton was subsequently made homeless, JaQuinn, who was said to have learning difficulties, was sent to live with the couple. This may have been an attempt by the boy's mother to afford him a better life than that offered by the homeless shelter that she and the other children moved into.

JaQuinn had been living with his godmother and her boyfriend for several months when Batson called 911 to say that the little boy had fallen out of an upper floor window. By the time the paramedics arrived, Batson had changed her story to say that her godson had missed a step and fallen down the stairs.

The first responders who attended the scene cried when later giving their testimony in court, saying that they had found JaQuinn, clearly having been subjected to unspeakable cruelty, in full arrest in the hallway of the defendants' home.

JaQuinn was kept on life support for two weeks before he died of his injuries. He had been subjected to a hideous catalogue of torture, including blunt force trauma to his head, and he died from a 'pancreatic laceration caused by blows to his stomach that had the force of a car crash'.

'I love JaQuinn so much,' said Batson in her first statement to the police. 'I'm devastated that it's not my child, first of all, and it happened in my care. I'm really feeling real bad about this situation.'

But it was quite clear that the toddler's injuries could not have occurred as the result of a fall, as claimed by Batson, and JaQuinn's caregivers were put on trial for his murder.

Batson claimed that the various burn marks on JaQuinn's body were the result of an accident in the bathroom. She told the court that he had stepped into hot water when she had briefly left the room. But trauma nurse practitioner Christine Biggie, who gave evidence about the injuries she observed on JaQuinn's body when he first arrived at the ER, testified that the burns were only on the tops of his feet, not on the bottom, where they would have been if he had stepped into the water.

Biggie had also noted multiple bruising, cuts and marks all over his face and body, at various stages of healing, some of which were open wounds, and some partially healed with bits of skin missing. She reported that he was very thin, with a swollen, distended abdomen.

Philadelphia Police Captain, James Clark, reported that there were 'numerous assaults to the body, by fists, through kicks and also some type of unidentified object.

Also, numerous burns to his legs, feet and buttocks from a blowtorch that the family had.'

§

A crucial witness was the neighbour who shared a kitchen and bathroom with Batson and King, who had heard Batson calling JaQuinn 'this little motherfucker' and 'this little nigger' on many occasions. He gave video-taped testimony of the abuse he had heard, by night and day, of whipping, yelling and screaming, which he could hear above the loud music Batson was playing. This took place at least four times per week, but sometimes twice a day, with Batson yelling at JaQuinn to shut up, to move his hands, and to stop crying. The neighbour agonised over what he heard, but admits he also put on loud music to try and shut out the sound.

On at least one occasion, when his girlfriend was upset by the screams coming from Batson and King's home, the neighbour knocked on their door and said that 'it' had been going on for a long time. Batson said she would turn her music off, and the incident ended, only for the noise to begin again the next day.

The neighbour sent a text to his landlord two weeks before JaQuinn was fatally injured, hoping that the landlord might intervene, though he didn't report what he heard to the police. His text was reminiscent of the way many bystanders must feel when they want to help the victim, but don't want to interfere. 'I ain't tryna get involved in other people's matters. But this woman beats her kid nonstop for hours. Shit just don't seem healthy to me'. He also checked the Department of Human Services website to find out how to anonymously report someone for suspected child abuse.

§

The prosecutor in the case was Assistant District Attorney Bridget Kirn. She said: 'He was small and he was frail and he was brave. He didn't have that many words, but *he could feel pain and he did.*' This indicates that she felt the perpetrators couldn't relate to the fact that their little victim was a human being, suffering terrible agony at their hands.

The attorney said that JaQuinn's ordeal began almost as soon as he entered the home shared by Batson and King. Marcus King, whilst confessing that he had hit JaQuinn on occasion, told the court that Batson was the 'enforcer' and 'disciplined' him at least every other day. He said he felt the beatings were sometimes excessive and that he occasionally tried to intervene. King also testified that he had tended JaQuinn's burns by running them under cold water, which caused his skin to peel off. He then dressed the wounds with cream and gauze. The pair had considered taking the little boy to the hospital, but were concerned about being arrested due to the nature of JaQuinn's injuries.

The three-year-old was beaten from head to toe, with fists, belts, shoes and hairbrushes. Batson also dragged a metal hair pick (a type of Afro comb with sharp teeth) across his skin. One of the excuses given for beating JaQuinn was that he sometimes touched things (presumably household objects) that he wasn't supposed to.

The boiling water that Batson poured on JaQuinn's feet and legs caused second degree burns and terrible swelling which meant he couldn't wear shoes and was rendered incapable of walking.

Court records state that on the night before he was taken to hospital, JaQuinn was having difficulty getting to sleep, and kept trying to get out of bed. Batson therefore chose to beat him, and after this beating, he allegedly went to sleep.

DA Kirn remarked that she felt Batson was 'evil' to commit such atrocities and that she was not surprised that the accused woman showed no remorse for her crimes. Even when photographs of JaQuinn's tortured body were shown, Batson was dry-eyed and unemotional, but she sobbed for herself when the jury returned the guilty verdict.

DA Kirn tried to press for a conviction for first degree murder, due to the relentless torture meted out to the defenceless child. This would have carried a sentence of life without parole. However, as deliberate intention to kill could not be proved (as in most 'tortured to death' cases), the prosecution had to be content with murder in the third degree and its lighter sentences. A torturer who puts their victim through hell before they die is usually sentenced more leniently than a person who, for example, shoots someone with intent to kill and they die instantly. Bridget Kirn said that what Batson did to JaQuinn was cruel and lacked any human capacity.

§

In their report, published in the aftermath of the tragedy in January 2012, the Department of Public Welfare found that there had been communication with the Brewton family prior to JaQuinn's murder, but that following the break up of the family, his mother did not know the exact address at which her three year old son was living, and that when questioned in March 2011, four months before her son's death, she said that she had not seen him since December 2010. The Department of Human Services failed to follow this up by filing a missing person's report with the police. This could have potentially saved JaQuinn's life, as a police officer approached Batson on the street just three days before the murder, having concerns about the boy's appearance. Had JaQuinn been on their missing person's file, the police could have intervened.

§

Nadera Batson was convicted of third degree murder, conspiracy to commit murder, child endangerment and possession of an instrument of crime, which was the small blowtorch that was used to burn JaQuinn on his bottom; a macabre tool in potty training. She was sentenced to 28 to 50 years in prison. Marcus King, who is 6ft 7ins tall and weighed 220lbs, pleaded guilty to third degree murder and was sentenced to 10 to 20 years.

An appeal lodged by Batson's legal team in 2015 was turned down with these words from the judge: 'In this unusually graphic and horrifying case, this Court took into account the ongoing nature both of the defendant's cruel behaviour and of the victim's suffering, and the defendant's hard-hearted refusal to access medical and supportive services or surrender the victim so that his suffering might be alleviated and his life spared.' And continuing: 'The grotesquery of the defendant's resort to torture via blowtorch suggests serious depravity, and to be frank, the defendant could easily have been sentenced to more time on other counts in recognition of that fact.'

I am unable to trace any information on the background of either Batson or King. Perhaps this would shed some light onto how they were capable of torturing JaQuinn without mercy.

Rest Safely in Peace, JaQuinn

When Did Child Abuse Begin?

JaQuinn was tortured to death in 2011, but the first recorded case of child abuse, as we now recognise it (although children were abused long before this), took place in the 1860-1870's.

Mary Ellen Wilson was born in Manhattan in 1864, and at just eighteen months old, when her widowed mother could no longer take care of her, Mary Ellen was fostered by Francis and Mary Connolly, who were paid well for her care. Mary Connolly took little interest in providing a welcoming home for the child, and began to abuse Mary Ellen by locking her in a closet whenever she went out.

At that time, no society to prevent cruelty to children existed.

When Mary Ellen was rescued at the age of nine, it was found that she had been confined to the closet for much of every day, burned with an iron, starved of food, affection, and companionship, whipped all over her body, including her head, and cut with scissors. Her foster mother was put on trial, and was sentenced to one year in jail.

As a direct consequence of Mary Ellen's case, the New York Society for the Prevention of Cruelty to Children was founded, the forerunner of all future child protection organisations. The NYSPCC still operates today.

Mary Ellen's story has a very happy ending. She was fostered by her rescuer, Etta Wheeler, married at the age of 24, had two daughters, and lived to the age of 92.

In the UK, prosecutions for cruelty to children have taken place since the 1880's, but the maltreatment death of Dennis O'Neill, whose story comes next, heralded the first public inquiry, and his landmark case helped to shape the modern day child protection system.

A Mouthful of Swede

Dennis O'Neill

03.03.32 - 09.01.45

aged 12 years & 10 months

Shropshire, England

I conclude this volume with the history of a young boy whose death instigated an overhaul of protection for 'looked after' children in the UK, at a time when child abuse was barely acknowledged. His name is Dennis O'Neill, and he died on a farm in rural Shropshire on 9th January 1945.

His little brother Terence, who witnessed Dennis' suffering, and received his own share of abuse, published a book in 2010, dedicated to his brother, entitled *Someone To Love Us*. I cannot hope to equal Terry's telling of their story, and so I include here just a few pages of what I learned about Dennis, largely from reading his brother's book.

§

Dennis lived in Newport, South Wales with his seven siblings, and parents who struggled to cope with the demands of their large family. The children were neglected, for which their parents were ordered to pay a fine of £3. Unable to pay, Mr and Mrs O'Neill were sent to prison for a month, and the younger children were sent to various places to be looked after, eventually to be placed with foster families. Following spells in homes where they were shown affection, and importantly to growing children, given plenty of food to eat, 12 year old Dennis and 9 year old Terry found themselves far from home, at the remote Bank Farm, in Shropshire's Hope Valley, under the care of Reginald and Esther Gough.

§

At first, the Goughs treated the youngsters satisfactorily, and the boys enjoyed helping out on the farm during the summer holidays, and after their chores, they were allowed free time to play in the fields or in one of the pools of water around the village.

Their first job of the day was to walk to a distant field, wade through the bracken, catch hold of the Goughs' two horses (often having to chase them up and down the meadow, as the horses didn't want to be caught), and walk them back towards the stables to feed them with hay. Their next task was to shoo the cattle into the milking shed, and finally to feed the hens and gather their eggs. These first few weeks were a comparatively happy time for the boys; Mr Gough even took them fishing one day, and taught them how to tickle trout, and Mrs Gough showed them how to make rugs out of rags.

Gradually though, Dennis and Terry began to see a much less pleasant side to their carers. Mr Gough in particular was unpredictable, and the boys started to get the blame for unfortunate events, such as when a calf or a chicken died.

The boys slept in an unfurnished attic, with just a straw mattress and an old blanket between them, and were expected to survive on two slices of bread and margarine three times a day, whilst their foster parents enjoyed hearty meals of rabbit stew with potatoes, or chicken soup.

§

When summer came to an end, and Dennis and Terence began walking to Hope Village School, they still had to work on the farm both before and after lessons. And in addition to their existing tasks, they now had to clean out the cowshed and the farm yard. But as autumn set in, the boys' tasks multiplied further, and became increasingly hard to do in the colder weather. A particularly tough job was tramping into the woods and collecting firewood. When their shoes wore out, they were supplied with clogs which caused blisters, and, given only short trousers to wear, they suffered the agonies of severely chapped legs and chilblains.

§

The first deliberately cruel incident the boys witnessed was when Mr Gough shut himself in the stable with the two horses and a pitchfork, and, outside in the yard, Dennis and Terence could hear the animals' terrified screaming. After the door was opened and Mr Gough went away, they saw the blood spattered stable, the gashes on the horses' backs, and the bloody pitchfork.

Shortly afterwards, a calf died, and the youngsters were blamed, and told they were to receive 'stripes' to teach them a lesson, which Gough delivered via a long thin stick onto the palms of their hands.

Only the next day, Terry accidentally dropped an egg, and earned himself another six strokes on the hand. The pattern was now set. For the slightest misdemeanour, real or imagined, the amount of 'stripes' due on any given day would be totalled up by their foster carers, and administered after the boys' evening feast of bread and margarine.

From this point on, Gough seemed to be permanently furious with Dennis and Terry, and relished every opportunity to punish them. And in a deliberate act of cruelty, Gough terrified the boys at Halloween, by draping himself in a white sheet and 'haunting' them.

As the November days wore on, the bitter cold and lack of food made the boys grow weaker, and yet they still had to work as hard as ever. By this time, both Dennis and Terry were losing weight and starving, but if they tried to sneak a little extra food from the Goughs' kitchen, they were usually found out and punished. Dennis was so desperate he even tried to suck milk from the cows' udders. At night, their agonising chilblains kept them awake, as they struggled to keep warm under their shared blanket. The bad cold that Dennis had developed at the beginning of winter, now turned into a persistent chest infection, and though he was kept off school, he was still expected to carry on the laborious tasks on the farm.

§

On 20th December 1944, after Dennis and Terry had been forced to clean the farmhouse and make up a cosy fire, a woman from Newport social services called at their foster home. The visit had been delayed due to uncertainty as to which authority (either Newport in Wales where the boys came from and had initially been placed in foster care, or

Shropshire where they now lived), was responsible for such visits.

Both boys were non-committal in their answers to the visitor, not complaining that they were hungry and overworked, as they couldn't be sure they wouldn't be sent on somewhere worse, or that if they stayed where they were they might suffer even more brutal treatment at the hands of the Goughs. Nonetheless, the woman, Miss Edwards, was concerned about how thin Dennis was and the dark circles under his eyes, and she instructed Mrs Gough to take him to the doctor, saying her expenses would be paid, on top of the money they already received. This was news to the boys. They now realised their foster parents were paid to care for them, and could easily have afforded to buy them shoes, a coat, and enough food to keep them strong and healthy. They discovered there was also pocket money allocated for them, which they had never been given. Although they didn't betray the Goughs by telling Miss Edwards about their cruelty, Esther Gough was not satisfied and threatened them with yet another beating. The visit to the doctor never materialised. It was later discovered that Miss Edwards had recommended their removal, but this was delayed, largely due to the Christmas holiday period. And not in time to save Dennis.

§

By Christmas Eve, the youngsters' hands were macerated by one hundred strikes each on their palms. Their bodies were covered in bruises and infectious sores, and they had septic ulcers on their feet. Neither boy could move without pain shooting all over his body. On Christmas Day they received a pack of playing cards and some cigarette cards, and were served their usual two slices of bread and margarine while the Goughs tucked into roast chicken with all the trimmings.

January 1945 brought snow and ice to Bank Farm, and the underfed O'Neill brothers shivered uncontrollably as they broke the ice on the water troughs so the animals could take a drink. When Mr Gough ordered Dennis to have a bath in the water trough and insisted he remove his clothes, it was the beginning of the end for the emaciated and starving boy. Terry experienced the same thing, and describes the agony of the blood returning to his freezing body. Dennis was slowing down, always on the verge of passing out, and yet he was made to stand at the table while the others ate their meal and he was given nothing. Gough shouted at Dennis constantly, and now devised a new torture; locking him in a narrow cupboard for hours at a time. Terry underwent the same punishment so he knew how frightening it felt to be locked away in the dark.

On 8th January, both boys were looking forward to getting back to the warmth and predictability of school. But Dennis was not permitted to attend, because Mrs Gough wanted him to gather wood for the fire. Dennis knew there was no dry wood to be had, but his foster mother was having none of it, and she forced him outside on an impossible search.

When Terry returned from school, Mrs Gough informed him that his brother had been stealing food. The starving boy's crime? Taking a bite from a swede in the Goughs' pantry. And when Mr Gough, who had been away from the farm all day, came home that evening, Dennis was in terror of what awaited him.

Firstly, both boys were made to stand and watch the Goughs eat soup and bread while they had nothing. Then came Terry's share of 'stripes' on his hands. By the time he turned to Dennis, Mr Gough had built up to a frenzy, accusing the boy of stealing, and refusing to bring firewood. He ordered Dennis to remove his clothes, and forced him outside into the freezing yard. When he was allowed back indoors, Mr Gough punched him fully in the face, and made the naked boy bend over a wooden pig bench. Gough tied Dennis to the bench with rope and beat him mercilessly with a stick, while the boy screamed in agony. Terry was sent to bed, and the beating went on.

Eventually, Dennis crawled into bed beside his brother, icy cold and crying uncontrollably. After a time, his torturer came up to the attic and punched Dennis repeatedly in the chest for making too much noise. Throughout the night, Terry could hear his brother's muted moans of anguish, and feel his nails clawing into the skin of his back as Dennis spent the hours of darkness in unimaginable pain and distress.

Terry did not know until a few days later, that his big brother had died during that dreadful night. It is almost impossible to read Terry's account of Dennis' final hours without tears of sorrow and anger. We are not usually privy to the death throes of a tortured 12-year-old.

§

The next morning, after instructing Terry to say that he had thumped his brother in the chest while they were in bed, Esther Gough eventually called for the doctor. Terry was amazed when he was given proper food to eat that day; vegetable soup for lunch and fried eggs for tea. He didn't dare to sneak up and see Dennis, and was told to sleep in another room that night.

The following day, Dennis was taken away on a stretcher, and the police took a still unsuspecting Terry to ask him some preliminary questions, and then drove him to hospital. A few days later, Dennis' death was reported in the newspapers, and another patient bluntly told Terry that his brother was dead. Following a post mortem, the cause of death was given as acute cardiac failure caused by violence to his chest and back, while in a state of under-nourishment due to neglect.

§

The Goughs' trial took place in February of that same year, and at ten years old, Terence O'Neill gave courageous and honest witness testimony.

Reginald Gough was found guilty of manslaughter and sentenced to six years in prison, and Esther Gough was convicted of neglect and sentenced to six months. Following a public outcry, by many accounts (although it is not mentioned by Terry in his book), the appeals court changed Reginald Gough's conviction to murder, and increased his sentence to ten years.

The case prompted a landmark Home Office Inquiry led by Sir Walter Monckton, and its findings highlighted the lack of communication between the two authorities responsible for the care of the O'Neill brothers. The report led to a reform of the care of 'looked after' children, and instigated the implementation of the 1948 Children's Act.

Dennis' and Terence's story highlights many of the pertinent factors in child maltreatment. Both boys were abused, but one was singled out more than the other. Violence began on a relatively small scale, as a form of discipline/punishment, then increased in frequency, intensity and sadism. It was accompanied by denying the boys adequate food, warmth, and medical attention. They were set impossible tasks, and kept in a state of uncertainty as to what might happen next. There was also some input from the authorities, who ironically were planning to remove the boys from the Goughs.

We have no information as to whether the Goughs themselves had been subjected to violence as children, but we do know that Reginald Gough had history; he had been convicted of assaulting Esther and she had left him in July 1942, only four months after marrying him. Although she did not follow it through, and later went back to him, she had applied for a separation order on the grounds of persistent cruelty.

Another aspect of the case is the financial benefit of fostering the O'Neill brothers. Money appeared to be tight on the farm, and with trampled or failing crops, and animals dying unexpectedly, the Goughs almost certainly felt under financial pressure. But they found a way to ensure that fostering two children could prove very profitable. With their diet of bread and margarine, and not enough clothes or footwear to keep them warm, little of the income gained from the arrangement filtered down to their charges, who were effectively used as slave labour.

§

Terence O'Neill's book goes on to give the fascinating story of his life after he left Bank Farm. He survived his harsh upbringing and raised his own family, with grandchildren and great grandchildren being added as the years go by. Now well into his 80's, it is clear that Terry never forgot his big brother, and the love expressed on his Facebook page hints at the well beloved great-grandfather that Dennis could also have become.

Reading Terence O'Neill's book made me doubt anew my place as storyteller of these harrowing cases. Compared to Terence O'Neill, and other family members of the tortured children, what do I know personally of how it feels to be touched by such pain and fear? Certainly no more or less than most people who live relatively comfortable lives.

But the last few pages of Terry's book gave me a little reassurance, as he laments the many deaths of tortured children that have occurred since Dennis' murder. Some of those children are included in this book, and some appear in Volume 2 of this series. It strengthens my resolve that we should never stop remembering the children, telling their stories, and looking for ways to improve their care.

Rest Safely in Peace, Dennis

Physical Discipline

Like many child murderers, Reginald Gough began his reign of terror by physically disciplining the O'Neill brothers. And then it escalated. Until within a few weeks, Dennis had been disciplined to death.

Over and over again, we see a murderer defending their actions by saying they were disciplining the child, such as Synthia Varela who murdered her son Omaree: *'I was disciplining him and I kicked him the wrong way'*. (I tell Omaree's story in Volume 2.)

And Isauro Aguirre, after he murdered Gabriel Fernandez, saying to the Arresting Officer: *'I spanked him'*. (You can find my telling of Gabriel's story on Amazon.)

Whilst we do not condone violence between adults, we seem to readily accept it when meted out to children, instead of looking for non-violent ways to guide them, such as short spells of time-out, withholding treats, and rewarding good behaviour. When calmly explained to the child, these methods can make them feel involved in the process and proud of their achievements.

Many loving and responsible parents who do smack their children, vigorously defend their right to do so. However, I feel that the longer we accept this as normal within our society, the more we also allow abusive parents to defend *their* behaviour.

If physical punishment has never begun, it *cannot* escalate to using the child as a punch-bag, or 'disciplining' them to the point of torture or death.

And crucially, if a child does not experience smacking, punching, kicking etc, it is much less likely that they will physically punish their own children, and the cycle of violence can be broken.

Heart-breakingly, a common reason given for this 'discipline' is that the child wet or soiled themselves, sometimes in reference to a child of less than one year old. A huge number of cases of torture seem to stem from the potty training stage. Yet terrifying a child is almost a guarantee that they will soil themselves. They are then caught on a treadmill of fear and punishment.

Although 70 countries have now followed the lead of Sweden in banning corporal punishment in the home, England and the USA seem likely to permit parents to physically punish their children for the foreseeable future.

That is the last of the children's stories, though not quite the end of the book. I know my books are not easy to read, so thank you for still being with me.

So what motivates me to write the children's stories? There are many reasons, and just as you may have, I've encountered many of life's ups and downs, having lived with abuse, depression, loss and grief.

But nothing prepared me for this:

Working alongside a colleague, I confided in her that though only in their early 30's, my older sister's two sons had recently died. She sympathised, and then said: "When my grandson died ..." Not surprised that she was visibly upset, I asked her more about Marc, and she told me that it had been in the newspapers at the time. I didn't interrupt her as she explained the dreadful circumstances of the seven-year-old's death.

His own mother had murdered him.

The more we talked, the more angry I felt that the system had not listened to her warnings, and had failed to protect Marc and his siblings.

Eventually, after discovering how horrifically frequently this happens, I realised that there was something I could do. By writing the children's stories, I could reach out to people, and play my part towards prevention. That's why I appreciate you so much.

Please don't feel bad about reading, and perhaps 'enjoying', my books. Only by making ourselves aware of what is happening behind closed doors can we hope to protect the 27 children who are abused to death each week in the US, and the 2 per week who are murdered in the UK.

> If you've been moved by the children's stories and would like to help me raise awareness, a **star rating or review** for this book enables new readers to find my books.

And I'd love to hear from you, so if you have any comments or suggestions, please get in touch:

jessicajackson@jesstruecrime.com

JESSICA JACKSON

Help To Protect Children ...

Please review in your usual way, or the QR code or link will help you to get back to the book's page:

mybook.to/Abused-To-Death-1

Then scroll waaay down
until you see Write a Review
(usually on the left side)

> Reviews help to spread awareness of abuse.
> Just a star rating or a few words is enough.

If you prefer, there are direct 'Easy Review Codes' at the back of this book, which take you where you need to be.

This book is dedicated to the memory of:

*Peter, Sylvia, Kristy, Amy, Jeanette,
Michael, JaQuinn & Dennis*

Your Next Book in the Series

Are you ready for more stories like these?

Volume 2 covers eight more cases, including the stepdaughter of serial killers, Fred & Rose West.

Find your copy in your usual way or:

Just scan this code:

Or use this link:
mybook.to/Abused-To-Death-2

Join Us On Facebook

Want to connect with me and join a community of people who want to prevent child abuse?

I honour the murdered children on my Facebook page, and if you'd like to come and say 'Hi' on one of my posts, it'd be great to see you there.

You may wish to **Follow Me & Share** my posts.

Just scan this code:

Or use this link:

https://www.facebook.com/AbusedToDeath/

Or within Facebook, type into the search bar:

Jessica Jackson – Writer Against Abuse

Hello (again!) from Jess

Would you like to **join my Readers' List**, by picking up your free ebook overleaf?

And would you please do me a great favour?

*Because my books are so sad, I double-check that you want to join my Readers' List, and so you'll receive a quick email from me, to ask you to **confirm your place**.*

> *Can you please reply either **Yes or No** to this email? It only takes a few seconds but is **incredibly** helpful to me.*

If you don't receive the email almost instantly, please check Junk/Spam – I can't add you without your reply.

Thank you; I really appreciate this.

Readers' List Benefits

Members get special offers, along with each new release at the subscriber price. And if you'd like to be more involved, you can **suggest children to include**, give your input on cover design, and lots more.

> *I'm always interested in what my readers think, and so on the day after you've confirmed your place and joined us, I'll email you with the question:*
>
> *"ARE THEY MONSTERS?"*
>
> *I'd love to include your opinion in my readers' poll.*
>
> *Then I'll leave you in peace for a while!*

So, get your free ebook overleaf, and thank you in advance if you decide to join us.

ABUSED TO DEATH VOLUME 1

Pick Up Your Free E-Book and Join Us!

Isaiah Torres was just six years old when he was abused to death in the most appalling way.

Pick up your copy of your free ebook

Just scan this code:

Or use this link:
https://BookHip.com/VNGMZJJ

Then be sure to click Yes or No on the quick email I'll send to confirm your place – it looks like this:

Yes thanks, I'd love to join, Jess

OR

No, I won't join just now, Jess

Find All My Books on Amazon

Find them in your usual way, or you can …

Search Amazon for:

Abused To Death by Jessica Jackson

Or scan this code:

Or use this link:

viewbook.at/abused-series

If you wish, you can also **Follow** me on Amazon.

Don't Miss A Thing

Pick up your free ebook:

Just scan this code:

https://BookHip.com/VNGMZJJ

And reply to your Yes or No email

Follow me on Facebook:
https://www.facebook.com/AbusedToDeath/

Follow me on Amazon:
viewbook.at/abused-series

*(Make sure your Settings in **Communications / Preferences in your Amazon account** are set to receive info about new releases.)*

Easy Review Codes

Scan the code to get to the review page

*It's quick & easy – just a star rating
or a few words is all it takes*

**For Amazon.com
(US, NZ, SA, etc)**

For Amazon in the UK

For Amazon in Canada

For Amazon in Australia

Or find it in your usual way

Thank you very much x

Acknowledgments

With grateful thanks to:

- Jackson and Rick who sustained me with emotional & technical support, and chocolate.
- My sisters, who constantly encouraged me, saying: "Keep going. Do it for the children".
- All my subscribers, especially my incredible Advanced Readers Team.
- True crime writers Ryan Green & Rob Keller, who enabled me to reach my first readers, including Sharon Wilson who wrote:

> "I have just finished reading your book and it will stay in my heart and mind for ever. Your telling of her story was haunting. Please keep doing this very important work."

Six weeks later, Sharon died from coronavirus, and along with the children in this volume, my book is dedicated to her.

… JESSICA JACKSON

Selected Resources

For Peter, Sylvia, Kristy and Amy

Blue Eyes
Peter
Connelly
London, UK
aged 1
Died 2007

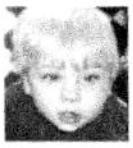

Nasty, brutish and short: the horrific life of Baby P
Nina Lakhani - independent.co.uk - 16.11.08

The catalogue of failures in Baby P's care
Caroline Gammell - telegraph.co.uk - 01.12.08

Serious Case Review - Peter Connelly
Haringey Safeguarding Children Board - 2010

Get Me Out Of Here
Sylvia
Likens
Indiana, USA
aged 16
Died 1965

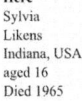

Looking back on Indiana's most infamous crime
Sam Stall - indianapolismonthly.com - 21.10.15

The Murder of Sylvia Likens as told over 50 years ago
Will Higgins - Retro Indy Star - 08.10.18

Torture Mom - Ryan Green
True Crime Novel - Ryan Green Publishing - 2018

A Family Christmas
Kristy
Bamu
London, UK
aged 15
Died 2010

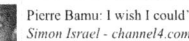

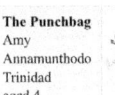

Pierre Bamu: I wish I could've died before Kristy
Simon Israel - channel4.com - 01.03.12

Revealed: The Torture Chamber Flat
James White - dailymail.co.uk - 01.03.12

A staggering act of depravity and cruelty
Agency staff - mirror.co.uk - 25.09.12

The Punchbag
Amy
Annamunthodo
Trinidad
aged 4
Died 2006

Girl 4, raped and buggered to death
Radhica Sookraj - Trinidad & Tobago News Forum - 17.05.06

Emily's (Amy's) granny: Thank God it's all over
Cecily Asson - archives.newsday.co.tt - 02.03.12

Baby Amy murder trial - Marlon King to hang
Sascha Wilson - guardian.co.tt - 02.03.12

Selected Resources continued

For Jeanette, Michael, JaQuinn and Dennis

Homeschool
Jeanette
Maples
Oregon, USA
aged 15
Died 2009

Cries for help for Jeanette Maples got no answer
Susan Goldsmith - The Oregonian - 02.01.10

Sister fills in disturbing details
Karen McCowan - Register-Guard - 18.02.11

Judge unseals search warrant affidavit
Janie Har - The Oregonian - 07.09.11

Fit For A Mother's Love
Michael
Dickinson
Cumbria, UK
aged 7
Died 2000

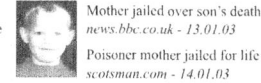

Mother jailed over son's death
news.bbc.co.uk - 13.01.03

Poisoner mother jailed for life
scotsman.com - 14.01.03

Serious Case Review - Michael Dickinson
Cumbria Child Protection Committee - March 2004

Blowtorch
JaQuinn
Brewton
Philadelphia,
USA
aged 3
Died 2011

Woman convicted of murder in death of toddler
Mike Lyons - westphillylocal.com - 14.08.13

Guilty verdict in torture, murder of child, 3
Mike Newall - inquirer.com - 12.08.13

Nadera Batson Appeal - Superior Court of Pennsylvania
Judges Stabile, Jenkins and Musmanno - courtlistener.com - 23.06.15

A Mouthful of Swede
Dennis
O'Neill
Shropshire, UK
aged 12
Died 1945

Someone To Love Us - Terence O'Neill
Harper Element - 2010

Overview of Monckton Report - Dennis O'Neill
Therapeutic Care Journal - 2011

Child Murder - The real story behind Agatha Christie's The Mousetrap
Aileen O'Brien - mirror.co.uk - 13.11.15

Selected General Resources

Beyond Blame	Peter Reder et al	1993	Routledge
Parents Who Kill	Carol Anne Davis	2009	John Blake
Out of the Darkness	Shelman & Lazoritz	1999	Dolphin Moon Publishing
hsinvisiblechildren.org	angelizdspace.com		abuseangelswixsite.com
findagrave.com	whatdotheyknow.com		murderpedia.org
library.nspcc.org.uk	actionagainstabuse		National Case Review Repository
Child Deaths due to Abuse or Neglect		2019	NSPCC Information Service
History of Child Protection in the UK		2018	NSPCC Learning
Children and Violence		1997	UNICEF Innocenti Digest 2
Child Maltreatment Deaths in Rich Nations*		2003	UNICEF Innocenti Report 5
Hidden in Plain Sight		2014	UNICEF
A Familiar Face		2017	UNICEF
Child Abuse and Neglect Fatalities (USA) 2017		2017	Child Welfare Information Gateway
Child Maltreatment (USA) Full Report 2017		2017	The Children's Bureau
Child Maltreatment		2016	World Health Organisation

Disclaimer

My aim is to tell the children's stories with a combination of accuracy and readability, to heighten awareness of child torture and murder, and to explore ways of preventing further tragedies. I have relied on the factual information available to me during my research, and where I have added characters or dramatised events to better tell the stories, I believe I have done so without significantly altering the important details. If anyone has further information about any of the cases, particularly if you knew the child and have anecdotes to share about their life, I would be delighted to hear from you. Likewise, whilst every attempt has been made to make contact with copyright holders, if I have unwittingly used any material when I was not at liberty to do so, please contact me so that this can be rectified at:

jessicajackson@jesstruecrime.com

Printed in Great Britain
by Amazon